Bark Canoes

Bark Canoes

The Art and Obsession of Tappan Adney

JOHN JENNINGS

Photographs by John Pemberton

Published in association with The Mariners' Museum

FIREFLY BOOKS

A FIREFLY BOOK

Published by Firefly Books Ltd. 2004

Publisher Cataloging-in-Publication Data (U.S.)

Jennings, John, 1941-
    Bark canoes : the art & obsession of Tappan Adney / John Jennings ; photographs by John Pemberton.—1st ed.
Published in association with The Mariners' Museum.
[152] p. : ill. (chiefly col.) ;   cm.
Includes bibliographical references and index.
Summary: Profile of the life and work of Edwin Tappan Adney, whose historically accurate canoe models preserved the history of Native bark canoe construction. Features photographs of 110 canoe models with captions explaining the source, building techniques and materials used for each canoe.
ISBN 1-55297-733-1
1. Adney, Tappan, 1868-1950. 2. Indians of North America — Boats . 3. Canoes and canoeing – North America. I. Mariner's Museum (Newport News, Va.).   II. Pemberton, John. III. Title.
623.8/ 29 22   E98.B6.J46 2004

National Library of Canada Cataloguing in Publication

Jennings, John, 1941-
    Bark canoes : the art & obsession of Tappan Adney / John Jennings ; photographs by John Pemberton.

Includes canoe models by Edwin Tappan Adney.
Co-published by Mariners' Museum.
Includes bibliographical references and index.
ISBN 1-55297-733-1

    1. Adney, E. Tappan (Edwin Tappan), 1868-1950. 2. Canoes and canoeing—Models—Pictorial works. 3. Indians of North America—Boats—Models—Pictorial works. I. Adney, E. Tappan (Edwin Tappan), 1868-1950. II. Mariners' Museum (Newport News, Va.) III. Title.

VM353.J46 2004   623.8'29   C2003-907455-2

Published in the United States in 2004 by
Firefly Books (U.S.) Inc.
P.O. Box 1338, Ellicott Station
Buffalo, New York 14205

Published in Canada in 2004 by
Firefly Books Ltd.
66 Leek Crescent
Richmond Hill, Ontario L4B 1H1

Developed and edited for The Mariners' Museum by Beverly McMillan
Interior design and art direction: Bob Wilcox
Cover design: Sari Naworynski

Printed in Canada by Friesens, Altona, Manitoba

The Publisher acknowledges the financial support of the Government of Canada through the Book Publishing Industry Development Program for its publishing activities.

For Nicola, companion in research, canoeing and life,
who has been surprisingly philosophical
about losing her dining room table to Adney
for the last two years.

Acknowledgements

This book began with a pilgrimage to The Mariners' Museum in 1998 while researching material for *The Canoe: A Living Tradition.* The idea for a book on the Adney models was planted during that first visit when I met John Pemberton, the Mariners' Creative and Visual Director, and was introduced to John Hightower, the President and CEO, and to Bill Cogar, then the Chief Curator of the Museum.

During my research trips for this book, the Museum staff was always welcoming and helpful, especially Claudia Jew, Greg Vicik, Melissa Duff, Lyles Forbes, Cathy Williamson, Lester Weber, Gregg Cina, Marc Nucup and Betty Zattiero. Beverly McMillan, the Publications Consultant, was an exacting editor and a delight to work with. At Firefly Books, Michael Worek, Charis Cotter and Bob Wilcox provided their usual expertise and enthusiasm.

The staff of the Canadian Museum of Civilization, the McCord Museum, the Peabody Essex Museum, the Peabody Museum of Archaeology and Ethnology at Harvard University, and the University of New Brunswick Archives were all extremely helpful. Michael Harrington and Janet Mason of the Canadian Conservation Institute were crucial in restoring the Adney models to their prime condition.

Ted Behne and Jim Wheaton provided valuable advice. Wheaton is currently writing the joint biography of Adney and his wife and has a vast store of knowledge on the Adney family.

I was helped enormously in writing the captions by three of Canada's leading experts on bark canoes: Rick Nash, Don Gardner and Jeremy Ward. I also received invaluable advice from Henri Vaillancourt, the legendary bark canoe builder.

Finally, this book owes much to my wife, Nicola, who enthusiastically shared much of the research.

Contents

Preface 9

Edwin Tappan Adney 11

Canoe Models 27

Canoes of the East Coast 28

Canoes of the Eastern Woodlands 50

Canoes of the Northwest 84

Canoes of Asia and South America 104

Canoes of the Fur Trade 120

Canoe Model Details 128

**How an Indian Birch-Bark
Canoe Is Made**
by E.T. Adney 130

The Birchbark Canoe 135

The Canoe Frontier 140

Glossary 146

Sources 147

Bibliography 148

Index 150

Maps

Native Peoples of Northern North America 8

Adney's Eastern Woodlands Map 134

Major Canoe Routes and Selected Forts 145

Native Peoples of Northern North America

Preface

It all began with the my father's canoeing stories. After flying Sopwith Camels in the First War, for a few years he was bowman for the Chief Forest Ranger of the Temagami District of northern Ontario. He looked very much like the Temagami rangers in the picture on page 138. My father instilled a love of wilderness in me that has only become more extreme over the years.

For the last twenty years, I have been deeply involved in the creation of the Canadian Canoe Museum in Peterborough, based on Professor Kirk Wipper's extraordinary collection of canoes and kayaks — by far the largest and most important in the world. It is enticing to think that Adney might have seen some of these craft in their previous locations.

In the mid-1990s, I first met Michael Worek of Firefly Books when he approached the Canoe Museum about doing a series of calendars featuring the collection. When he suggested creating a canoe book in collaboration with the museum, I was the logical one to take it on. I jumped at the idea with great enthusiasm and I was able to gather together eleven other authors to contribute to what has become *The Canoe: A Living Tradition*.

I decided that it was not possible to do such a book without making a pilgrimage to see the legendary Adney models at the Mariners' Museum and to look at his papers. I made my first trip there in 1998. I was utterly overwhelmed by seeing all the Adney models together, and equally overwhelmed by the richness — and chaos — of his papers.

From the moment my wife Nicola and I first arrived at the Mariners' we were treated with extraordinary kindness and generosity by all those we encountered. That first day, after seeing the models, I was introduced to the Mariners' chief photographer, John Pemberton. He showed me some photographs that he had taken of the Adney models and I realized that I was in the presence of someone who was technically very good, but who also brought a creative brilliance to his photography. I remember muttering that someone should do a book on these models and John saying something like, "well?" That was the beginning of this book. John arranged that I speak to John Hightower, president of the Mariners' Museum, who received me with great courtesy and enthusiasm. From that first day, it took a few years to confirm that the book would happen, but I like to think that it started with my first meeting with John Pemberton. I consider this book as much his as mine. I am in awe of his ability to choose just the right angle to shoot a model so that the images never lose their freshness.

After the terrible ordeal that Adney went through in finding a home for his cherished models and research papers, I think he would be content. His models were not properly appreciated in Canada; at the Mariners' Museum they are. Most of the models were sent in 2001 to the Canadian Conservation Institute in Ottawa, one of the foremost places in the world for the treatment of bark and skin. The models now look incredible. And Adney's papers have received a grant for proper cataloging. There still remain in those papers large areas of untapped information. I hope the publication of this book will add to an appreciation of the most extraordinary individual in the world of canoe scholarship.

Tappan Adney, artist and correspondent for *Collier's Weekly*
on the beach at Cape Nome, Alaska, during the gold rush, 1901.

Edwin Tappan Adney

The canoe models of Edwin Tappan Adney, universally recognized as the foremost scholar of the North American bark canoe, represent the distillation of a lifetime of research into the Native canoeing cultures of northern North America. Adney originally intended his collection of models to illustrate a major book on the subject. Sadly, he never completed that work, and his extraordinary models have remained in storage at the Mariners' Museum in Newport News, Virginia, for more than half a century, known only to a relative few. It is estimated that Adney constructed about 150 models of Native canoes during his lifetime. This volume presents the complete collection of Adney models at the Mariners' Museum — 110 in all — representing all major Native groups of North America who built bark canoes.

Tappan Adney was unquestionably the most important scholar the canoe world has known. Fortunately, his passion for Native canoe culture came at a time when it was still possible to gather information from elderly Native canoe builders and retired fur traders of the birchbark era. As a result, his research yielded an extraordinarily diverse and voluminous written record in addition to his models.

For Adney, building models was not a hobby or an appendage to some other enterprise. He believed that Native bark canoes, and knowledge about their construction, were fast disappearing. Therefore a collection of exact replicas at a consistent scale of 1 to 5 would be crucial for the preservation of this aspect of Native heritage.

When Adney began building, he was the only one in the world doing so, and even he was almost too late. During his 63 years of intermittent research, from 1887 to his death in 1950, much of the first-hand knowledge of bark canoes disappeared. Without Adney's vast collection of papers and the models he left as his legacy, a vital part of North American Native heritage might well have been irretrievably lost.

In a way, Tappan Adney was a tragic figure. He would probably be largely unknown today if someone else — Howard Chapelle — had not completed his great book

for him, because he never quite got around to the task. While the study of canoes was undoubtedly his great passion, he was all too easily distracted by his many other obsessions, including Native languages and ethnology, photography, painting and music. Adney read Greek, Latin, French and Maliseet, and spoke the latter fluently. The 10 boxes of his Native canoe material at the Mariners' Museum and the 88 boxes of his research records at the Peabody Essex Museum in Salem, Massachusetts, mostly on the subject of Native linguistics, attest to the depth of his scholarship. They also include material on Native culture, botany, astronomy and heraldry — a subject on which Adney would become one of North America's leading experts. He developed an abiding interest in birds as well, and was a charter member of the Explorers Club. His illustrations were used in museum publications, in Frank M. Chapman's *Handbook of Birds of Eastern North America* (first published in 1895) and in Theodore Roosevelt's *Good Hunting*. Combining the roles of journalist, artist and photographer, he wrote and illustrated *The Klondike Stampede*, about the Klondike gold rush. Appalled by the cruelty to horses he witnessed in the Klondike, he became a strong advocate for animal rights and lectured for the Society for the Prevention of Cruelty to Animals. Yet Adney's first love always remained the Native bark canoes, and their linguistic and cultural context.

EARLY YEARS

Tappan Adney was born in 1868 in Athens, Ohio. His father, W.H.G. Adney, was a professor of natural history at Ohio University and a Civil War veteran, having served as acting commander of the 36th Ohio Volunteer Infantry Regiment. His parents eventually went their separate ways; his mother, Ruth Clementine Shaw Adney, took both Adney and his sister, Mary, from their farm in Pittsboro, North Carolina, to New York City where, in 1883, Adney enrolled in the New York Art Students' League. Working in a law office during the day, he studied art in night school for the next three years under William Merritt Chase and Kenyon Cox. Adney's mother ran a boarding house in New York and it was there that Adney met his future wife, Minnie Bell Sharp, the daughter of the well-known Canadian horticulturist Francis Peabody Sharp. Minnie, who was independent and strong-minded, had come to New York from her childhood home of Woodstock, New Brunswick, to study piano and voice, and boarded with the Adneys. In her way, she was as unorthodox as Adney and they apparently soon fell in love. Minnie also had considerable musical ability; during most of the 1890s, she operated the Victoria Conservatory of Music in Victoria, British Columbia, and, later, the Woodstock School of Music.

In June 1887, at the age of 19, Adney decided to visit Woodstock. He probably made the trip either because Minnie was there at the time or because she had whetted his interest in the area. We know from his journal that he received a "warm welcome" at the Sharp home and that

his sister, Mary, was also visiting the Sharps at the time. In this period Adney seemed to be primarily interested in birds. In Woodstock he met Peter Jo, one of the last of the Maliseet canoe builders on the Saint John River. It was a meeting that would change Adney's life, for Peter Jo introduced Adney not only to Native canoe building, but also to Maliseet culture, which, off and on, Adney would study and document for the rest of his life.

Adney stayed almost two years in New Brunswick, from June 1887 to February 1889. During this time he lived for an extended period with Peter Jo and his family in order to learn the Maliseet language and to record and sketch the detailed building of a birchbark canoe — something that had never been done before. Under Peter Jo's tutelage, he also built his first birchbark canoe and his first bark canoe models. Adney later wrote in the draft preface for his planned canoe book that he had built

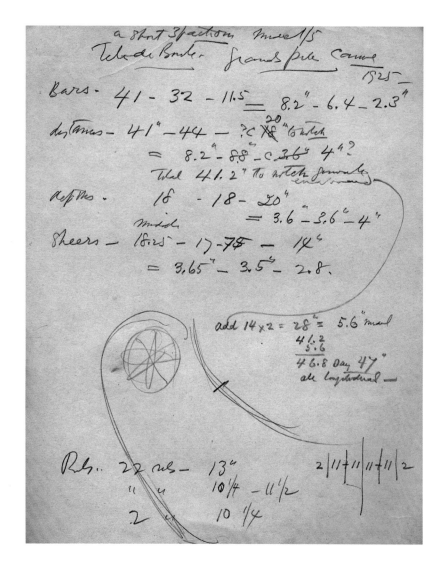

LEFT: A typical page of calculations for reducing a full-size canoe to a 1 to 5 scale model. These calculations relate to the Têtes de Boule fur trade canoe that Adney found at Grand Piles, Quebec (see #80, p. 127).

RIGHT: Frank Atwin, one of Adney's many Native sources of canoe building wisdom, seen here in the 1920s at age 80. Atwin was a Passamaquoddy builder from the Maine–New Brunswick region. This photograph shows him with a model of an ocean-going birch-bark canoe that he made in the 1890s. The model bears his personal mark, a tadpole, etched into the bark.

some models with Peter Jo, "including one of a one-fifth scale now in the American Museum [of Natural History]." He also noted: "We chose this scale and adhered to it as the smallest by which the details of technique such as the root-sewing could be worked in the original materials."

Peter Jo can be thanked for starting Adney on the path of preserving North America's bark canoe heritage. Already many forms of Native bark canoes were extinct, and there was, for instance, no example of a Montreal canoe, the largest of the fur trade canoes, in any museum in the world. Such watercraft had all settled back to earth, and no one seemed to care.

In 1890, the year after his sojourn with Peter Jo, Adney published a detailed description and sketches of the building of a Maliseet birchbark canoe in *Harper's Young People Supplement*. Another version appeared in *Outing* in May 1900. Up to this point, historical descriptions of Native canoes had been frustratingly vague, and no one had described or illustrated the building process in useful detail.

THE KLONDIKE

In 1897, 29 years old and still unmarried, Adney departed for the Klondike gold rush as a special correspondent for *Harper's Weekly* and the *London Chronicle*. Lugging his 5x7 long-focus Premo camera over the famous Chilkoot Pass linking southeastern Alaska with the Canadian Yukon, he sketched, photographed and recorded the gold rush. Adney wrote in a compelling but restrained style and demonstrated a wonderful eye for detail, both in his writing and in the sketches and photographs that accompanied his articles. *The Klondike Stampede,* first published in 1900, has become a classic.

TAPPAN ADNEY

The Klondike Stampede provides a unique reference to Adney as a canoeist. In a large canoe, Adney and a friend shot the gorge at the outlet of Lake Bennett, which links White Pass to the Yukon River. Adney's own account was understated, but fortunately the incident was observed by journalist J.B. Burnham of *Forest and Stream*, who described things quite differently:

One of the men was a slender six-footer, with a face wind-tanned the color of sole-leather ... His feet were moccasined, and his black hair straggled from under his red toboggan cap. Not only was his rig suggestive of the aborigine, but his every action proved him to be so thoroughly at home in his untamed environment that it is little wonder that at first glance I took him to be an Indian ... Adney was an expert at river navigation ... I heard some men calling out from the top of the canyon-like bank that the *Harper's Weekly* man was shooting the rapids. I ran across just in time to see the boat swept by with the speed of a bolt from a crossbow, leaping from wave-crest to wave-crest, and drenching its occupants with sheets of spray. Adney and

Brown were standing erect ... each wielding a single oar ... and from their masterly course it was evident that they had their boat well under control. It was all over in a small fraction of time. They had avoided by the narrowest of margins jagged boulders that it seemed impossible to pass, and in a slather of foam shot out into the smooth water below.

The Klondike Stampede contains only one detailed reference to Native canoes, and even great admirers of Adney acknowledge that he knew far more about eastern canoes than he did about western ones. Yet he was in the Klondike at a time when there were still many Native canoes being built. This reference and a sketch of Klondike and Tanana canoes in the Peabody Essex Museum make it clear that, even at this early date, he had begun to accurately document the craft.

THE OBSESSION

In 1899, at age 31, Adney, who had returned from the Klondike, married Minnie Bell Sharp in Woodstock. Then in 1900 he was off again, this time as a journalist for

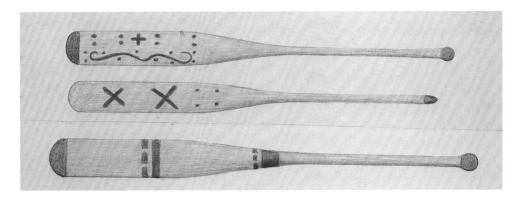

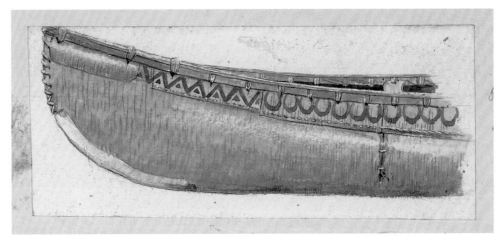

LEFT: Lithograph by Adney of two Maliseet hunters calling a moose. This illustration appeared in *St. Nicholas Magazine*.

TOP RIGHT: Drawing of three Cree paddles by Tappan Adney. The two shorter ones were women's paddles. Adney copied them from a 1782 sketch from the London office of the Hudson's Bay Company.

BOTTOM RIGHT: A drawing of a Penobscot canoe by Tappan Adney. John McPhee used this drawing for the cover of his book, *The Survival of the Bark Canoe*.

Collier's Weekly to cover the continuation of the Klondike gold rush at Nome, Alaska. When he returned he and Minnie Bell lived for a while in Flushing, Long Island, but they returned to Woodstock in the spring of 1902 for the birth of their first and only child, Francis Glenn Adney. He and Minnie spent the next seven years in New York City, she probably studying or teaching music, and he working as a freelance journalist and illustrator and, for a time, on the staff of the Museum of Natural History. Then, in 1907, they moved to New Brunswick where, among other preoccupations such as heraldry and custom bookbinding, Adney attempted without success to run his father-in-law's orchard business.

In 1915 he constructed on Sharp property near Upper Woodstock what he called his "bungalo," which resembled a sort of summer-camp building. Adney would use it only occasionally until the 1930s.

When World War One came, Adney was mustered into the Canadian Expeditionary Force at Valcartier, Quebec, on March 10, 1916. Curiously, he listed his son, Francis Glenn Adney, as his next of kin, rather than Minnie. He also gave his date of birth as July 13, 1872. At the time, Adney was 48; perhaps he needed to subtract four years from his age in order to be accepted for military service. He spent the next three years mostly at Canada's Royal Military College in Kingston, Ontario, as a lieutenant in the Royal Canadian Engineers, and became a Canadian citizen in May 1917. At the Royal Military College Adney was assigned to construct models of trench warfare for troop training. Used at training depots across Canada, his models reflected the most important evolutions in trench defenses on the Western Front. In January 1920, Major General Sir G.W. Gwatkin, Chief of Staff of the Canadian Army, wrote to the British War Office in London: "[Adney] was employed on … [models of trench warfare] for a considerable time under the Canadian Government, and he proved himself a genius … Better work than this I have never seen."

After the war Adney moved to Montreal, where he worked as a commercial artist specializing in works such as murals and heraldry at the rate of $3 an hour. Minnie remained in Woodstock, where she established herself as a piano teacher. Adney, too, spent quite a bit of time there. Meanwhile, to support his canoe obsession Adney existed mostly on commercial art contracts of one sort or another. For instance, for the Hudson's Bay Company headquarters in Winnipeg he and Adam Sherriff Scott painted two huge murals measuring 10 by 52 feet — one of the founding of Fort Charles (Rupert House) in 1668 and the other of Fort Garry in 1860. He painted the 10 provincial shields for the Canadian National Railway and completed a similar contract for Currie Hall at the Royal Military College. Other assignments included 66 armorials for the Champlain Room at the Chateau Frontenac in Quebec City and the armorials for the Osler Library at McGill University. Adney later designed the coat of arms for the Canadian College of Physicians and Surgeons.

As Adney settled into life in Montreal, his interest in Native bark canoes became more focused and he intensified his search for what remained of Native canoe culture. Since certain types of craft had already disappeared, his approach in some cases involved the reconstruction of canoes based on information gleaned from a detailed study of Native cultures and languages. Fortunately there remained a few active Native bark canoe builders and several retired fur traders whom he was able to track down through the Hudson's Bay Company. The Adney papers at the Mariners' Museum are full of inquiries, detailed interviews and reports of visits to Native builders. He also relied heavily on early photographs, especially those of the Geological Survey of Canada, which used birchbark canoes well into the twentieth century.

For information on the fur trade Adney relied heavily on Louis Christopherson, a retired fur trader at North Bay, Ontario. In 1877 Christopherson had become a postmaster for the Hudson's Bay Company at Lake Barrière, an Algonquin settlement 50 miles east of Grand Lake Victoria, northwest of Ottawa. From 1885 to 1908 he worked there as factor and over the years supervised the building of many fur trade canoes. Christopherson died in 1928, only three years after they met. Adney also gathered a great deal of invaluable information while visiting the area around Grand Lake Victoria and Lake Barrière, which was one of the last active Native birchbark canoe building regions in North America.

Outspokenly contemptuous of most canoe art (except for the paintings of Paul Kane and Frances Hopkins), Adney's precise drawings of the canoes he encountered in his travels, and his copies of canoes from historical sources, became vital to this work. At some point during his Montreal years, however, Adney realized that his graphic documentation of Native bark craft had to be accompanied by the systematic building of models. Convinced that knowledge of canoe building was fast disappearing — a belief that was also at the root of his compulsion to record Native languages and legends — Adney believed that exact three-dimensional representation was the only way to guarantee that knowledge of all the different canoe types would be saved.

Also driving Adney's decision to build exact models was his belief that it was essential to actually construct a canoe in order to ensure that the craft could have been built as described in historical literature or by Native elders. Some of these men remembered building canoes, but others only recalled seeing them many years earlier. This approach enabled Adney to discount some early conjectures on the extinct Beothuk canoe of Newfoundland; he found that birchbark simply could not be shaped as some sources described.

During the 1920s Tappan Adney began construction of exact and consistent 1 to 5 scale models of all the important Native bark canoe types, based on detailed notes, drawings and photographs. He reasoned that models should be built for museums because so few canoes could be found in museums and, of those that had been collected, some were seriously flawed. Adney felt that, when museums finally did recognize the importance of preserving these canoes, there would not be many good specimens left. (On one occasion a Maliseet builder told Adney that he had sold one of his canoes to a museum, noting that it was such a poor specimen that he had been embarrassed to take money for it.) In addition, Adney knew that few museum people could distinguish good Native canoes from indifferent ones; there was almost no published material on the subject.

THE STRUGGLE FOR RECOGNITION

By the mid-1920s, Adney began sounding out possible publishers for his proposed manuscript on bark canoes, thus initiating 15 years of polite refusals or vague encouragements that came to nothing, first on the issue of a manuscript and later on the sale of the model collection as well. In 1925 Scribner's set the tone when an editor wrote Adney: "It is our impression that we could count on only a very limited audience for a work of this character." In 1930, Adney approached the Henry Ford Museum of Transportation and Industry, asking $25,000 for the model collection. By then, however, in the aftermath of the 1929 stock market crash, the Ford Museum was noncommittal and Adney did not pursue the proposal strongly. In 1931, a nearly destitute Tappan Adney approached the Smithsonian Institution, the Field Museum of Natural History in Chicago, and George Heye, Director of the Heye Foundation at the Museum of

How To Build a Bark Canoe

by Tappan Adney

This set of diagrams was published in Adney and Chapelle's *The Bark Canoes and Skin Boats of North America*. The original captions have been revised.

1

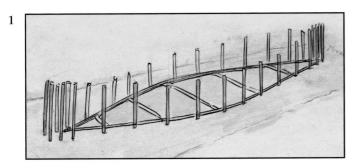

A gunwale frame is used to give the canoe its basic shape. Stakes are placed in the ground at regular intervals. In some areas, a building frame is used instead of gunwales.

2

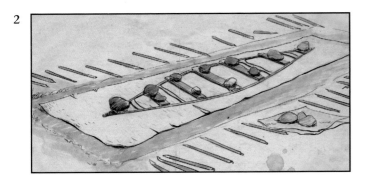

The stakes and the gunwales or building frame have been removed and laid aside. A single sheet of bark, with the outside of the bark on the inside, is aligned on a carefully smoothed bed. Then the gunwales or building frame are placed over the bark and weighed down with stones.

3

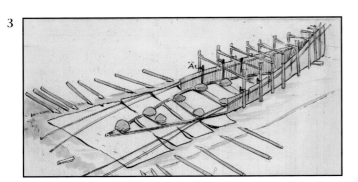

The bark is now shaped over the building bed and the stakes reinserted in their holes in pairs and tied across the canoe. Gores are cut in the bark as the canoe is shaped toward the ends. Part of the bark has been shaped here and secured between the stakes and long battens, held by sticks lashed to the stakes.

4

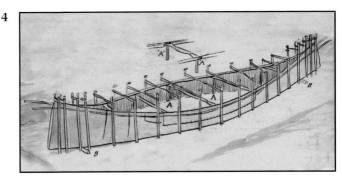

The bark has been shaped and the gunwales raised to sheer height. "A" indicates the sticks that determine the sheer of the gunwales. Blocks ("B") are placed under the ends to determine the rocker. The side panels are shown in place and the thwarts have been inserted. The side seams and gores are sewn and the stempieces (not visible) are sewn in place to form the ends. Double gunwales (inwale and outwale) are now in place. If the gunwales and thwarts have been used as a building frame, the sides will slope inward (tumblehome) once the ribs are in place. If a narrower building frame is used, the sides will flare.

5

The canoe is removed from the building bed and set on horses for complete sewing and shaping the ends. The canoe is now ready for the ribs to give it a final shape.

6

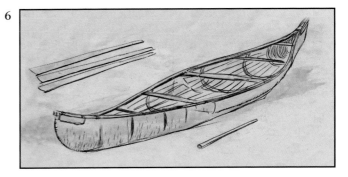

The cedar sheathing (upper left) is placed in the canoe, overlapping in the middle, and is held in place by temporary ribs (lower right). The wulegessis is in place and the canoe is ready to take its final shape. The ribs are inserted in pairs from the ends and tapped in place, their ends fitting firmly between the inwale and outwale with group lashing in the space between the ribs.

the American Indian in New York City. Heye was a legendary collector of Native artifacts; his acquisitions for the Museum of the American Indian eventually became the core of the Native canoe collection at the Canadian Canoe Museum in Peterborough, Ontario. Yet Heye refused both Adney's model collection and even a proposal for an article on Native bark canoes, and Adney fared no better elsewhere. The Smithsonian indicated that while the specimens were undoubtedly of much interest, it had no funds available. The Director of the Field Museum was more blunt. "The Field Museum is not interested in the canoes of birch or any other barks of America."

Undaunted, and seeking both financial help for the book and a buyer for the models, in 1936 Adney approached the Edison Institute of Dearborn, Michigan, and T.A. Crerar, the Canadian federal Minister of Mines and Resources, who oversaw Canada's national museums. (Adney had previously tried to gain a position at the National Museum in Ottawa but Crerar had turned him down flat.) Rejections of all these proposals are found in Adney's various papers; there were probably more.

Despite these frustrations, Adney at least knew that he was greatly respected where it really counted, among the great names in cultural anthropology and linguistics, in both Canada and the United States. It is clear, from his correspondence with men like Edward Sapir, Marius Barbeau and especially Diamond Jenness, that there was an easy familiarity and the mutual respect of intellectual equals. Edward Sapir, a brilliant linguist, was the first chief of the Geological Survey of Canada's division of anthropology, known internationally for his writing on the psychology of culture. Marius Barbeau was the founder of professional folklore studies in Canada, with nearly a thousand publications to his credit. Diamond Jenness was an anthropologist specializing in Inuit culture and Chief Anthropologist of the Canadian National Museum (later the Museum of Man and now the Canadian Museum of Civilization). While these three men were Adney's principal mentors, his papers are also full of correspondence with other experts in cultural anthropology and linguistics. The letters he received from all over North America are overwhelmingly enthusiastic and appreciative of Adney's research, acknowledging it as both unique and vital. The only exception was his effort to obtain information from Soviet sources about the bark craft of Siberia, which was met with a wall of silence.

In a letter to Sapir in 1925, Adney made a noteworthy comment. "I was glad to have in the form of [a] letter the expectation of the department [the Canadian National Museum] to publish [the] work that I have undertaken upon the subject of Bark canoes." By this time, Adney was clearly full of the thrill of the chase and reassured that his great canoe study was being taken seriously in high places. Unfortunately Sapir, who enthusiastically supported his research, soon left for the University of Chicago and his replacement, Marius Barbeau, would not make the same promise.

Adney's correspondence suggests that he was closest to Diamond Jenness. In 1940, in a moment of reflection, he wrote to Jenness, "I shall not soon forget how it was Barbeau and yourself whom I shall hold as largely if not entirely responsible for having instigated my attack on the Bark canoes, which I might not have made but for the encouragement given." The comment is revealing. Although Adney had begun building models in 1889, evidently it was much later, after World War One, that Jenness and Barbeau convinced him to embark on the documentation and crafting of models as key parts of his canoe research. Support for this conclusion appears in the draft preface of his canoe book, where Adney stated: "As the [canoe] material was accumulating from intensive research after about 1925 we resumed the construction of scale models ... by which we were able to discover fatal flaws in some otherwise plausible descriptions." In 1932 Adney commented in a letter to Jenness that about 100 canoe models were at McGill, with another 21 still in his possession. Thus it is clear that he had completed most of the models by this time.

Many letters passed between Adney and Jenness, most on technical matters such as the different components of Native red ocher or some aspect of Native anthropology. And it was usually to Jenness that Adney revealed his moments of discovery. On one occasion he related that one such epiphany came while he was playing with one of his Beothuk models in the bathtub:

A practical experiment in the bathtub with my Beothuk model, reveals the astonishing fact that even better than the Mi'kmaq, the gunwale at the low quarter is brought to water level with a wide margin of freeboard amidship ... I have a hunch that when the truth is known, the reason for the hump in the New Brunswick Mi'kmaq is for the better taking aboard of porpoises and seals.

Adney was alluding to the fact that, because of the rise amidships in the Beothuk and Mi'kmaq seagoing canoes, the craft could be leaned over 35° without shipping a drop of water. Thus, the near gunwale could be used as a fulcrum at the low quarter to drag in the hunter's quarry as others in the canoe leaned on the far gunwale for leverage. A simple feature, but one that could be discovered only by building an actual model of the craft. In his letter to Jenness Adney added that a Passamaquoddy chief had sent him a picture of a large Maliseet seagoing canoe made of a single sheet of bark and with a 42-inch beam, which was capable of taking in a 300-pound porpoise at the low quarter, something that Jacques Cartier had remarked upon with amazement in the 1530s.

THE MCGILL YEARS

Despite the encouragement he received from men like Jenness, during the 1920s in Montreal Adney lived a life of perhaps not so quiet economic desperation. It was during this decade that he became involved with McGill University's Strathcona Ethnological Museum, a connection that would be his one constant physical link with the museum world.

According to a rather fierce document entitled "Summary of Relations Between Edwin Tappan Adney and McGill University," Adney's involvement with McGill began with his son, Glenn, who came to McGill from New Brunswick in 1919 as a scholarship student in mathematics and physics. After graduate school at McGill, Glenn Adney switched to the Faculty of Music, where he achieved a reputation for brilliance. Following postgraduate work in physics at the University of Chicago, Glenn became a well-known pianist and band leader in Montreal.

Lionel Judah, curator of the McGill University museums, which included the Strathcona Ethnological Museum, first heard of Tappan Adney in 1926 from

This sketch by Tappan Adney was one of two preliminary sketches for the building of the five-fathom Express canoe (#120, p. 124), based on a Native model collected in 1870 by G.M. Dawson. The shape of the bow is typical of the Lake Temagami region.

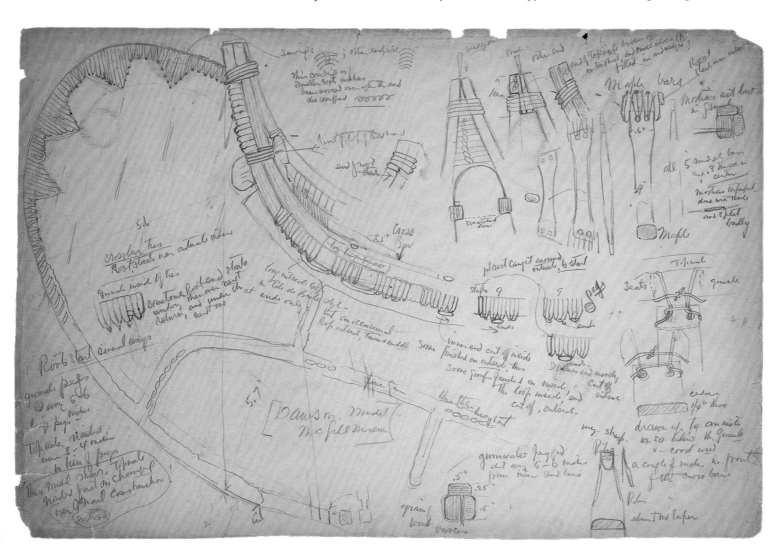

Adney's landlord, who was about to seize his canoe models for non-payment of rent on his apartment on Drummond Street. Judah offered to store the canoe models on exhibit in the museum to keep them safe from seizure, agreeing to notify the landlord if Adney attempted to remove them from the museum. Adney eventually paid off his debt, but the models remained at McGill, officially entered into the Loan Book on June 8, 1928. As Adney produced more models, they also were added to the McGill collection. And, unfortunately as it turned out, Judah would be Adney's closest contact in the museum world for the next decade.

Adney's financial situation continued to deteriorate. As the Canadian economy took a nosedive after 1929, so did Adney's prospects. By the early 1930s, Adney was in a desperate financial state. In the summer of 1930, on behalf of McGill, Judah had asked him to lead an expedition to the Missinaibi River in northern Ontario to sketch and photograph Native pictographs that had recently been reported on Little Missinaibi Lake. It was thought that these rock paintings had never been seen by Europeans. A large file on this expedition at the Peabody Essex Museum reveals much discussion of $91.60 in expenses Adney incurred for the trip — a considerable sum in the depths of the Depression, and a debt that Judah, and McGill, never paid. Adney was desperately poor; McGill, with its own finances stretched thin, was clearly utilizing his services for as little as possible.

In 1931 Lionel Judah again offered Adney a small commission, asking him to construct a model of a Maliseet hunter's camp and otter trap for the McGill museum. Judah reported to the museum that, when he had called on Adney to discuss the contract, he had found Adney and his wife "down and out" at their house in Verdun and greatly in need of money; in fact they were without food or heat. In these straits, Adney was only too happy to take what he thought was a down payment of $25 for his work. But there ensued an extraordinarily bitter dispute between Adney and the museum over this contract, which was revealing both of Adney's treatment by the museum and also of his extreme stubbornness. The dispute finally reached Sir Arthur Currie, Principal of McGill University and Canada's greatest World War One hero. Tucked away in an extensive official file on the subject is a letter from the Secretary of the Faculty of Medicine, Dr. J.C. Simpson. He had been asked to arbitrate Adney's complaint against Judah that he had received only a partial payment on his model hunter's camp and otter trap, rather than full payment as Judah alleged. The unreimbursed expenses for the Missinaibi expedition were another issue. Adney argued that he was being badly used, with Judah playing on his urgent need for funds. In his report Simpson wrote:

> It seems undoubtedly the fact that the models [the hunter's camp and otter trap] are worth many times the amount that Mr. Adney received. The point at issue seems to be that Mr. Adney claims that he would not under any circumstance have been willing to do work of this character at the rate of $5.00 a week, whilst Mr. Judah claims that, in view of his financial condition at the time, he was glad to do the work for even this small sum.

Underlying this situation was Adney's intense frustration that, because of his lack of university qualifications, he was not accorded the respect he felt was his due. And he was furious that the McGill museum thought it could throw him morsels and expect him to be grateful. Judah, for his part, seemed to be scrounging contracts for Adney to keep him from starving. The issue of the Maliseet models ground on for more than a decade; Adney pursued it relentlessly and even threatened a lawsuit.

Adney complained bitterly to a McGill trustee that he was being kept in a subordinate position as a "model-maker" and observed that, in Canada, museum staff seemed mainly interested in building walls to keep others out. It was very different, he said, in the United States, where talent was sought out and the atmosphere was more generous. It must have been galling for a man so respected by some of the greatest anthropologists and linguists of the time to be treated as an underling by the museum with which he had closest contact.

In the midst of this turmoil, in January 1932 Adney arranged for a loan of $500 from McGill, with his model collection as collateral. Shortly thereafter, in May, the museum appointed him an "Honorary Consultant," a title that gave him a degree of stature but no income. At the end of July he was forced to negotiate a further loan of $500, for a total of $1,000 borrowed at 6 percent interest for a term of seven years. If the loan remained unpaid at the end of that period, nonpayment would represent a "sale" of the models to McGill for the original loan amount plus interest due.

As the dispute over payment for the model camp and trap festered on, Adney accused Judah of "petty swindling" and Judah claimed that Adney was a master at twisting the facts. Finally, in February 1933, McGill had had enough and revoked Adney's honorary status. At the bottom of the letter terminating his honorary status,

Adney noted that this was Judah's way of getting even. Yet he also commented, with great satisfaction, that the McGill Museums Committee was so annoyed at Judah for paying Adney so little for his work, and for refusing to reimburse his expenses from the Missinaibi expedition, that the committee had deprived Judah of his post as curator of the McGill Ethnology Museum.

In January 1933, in the midst of his troubles with McGill, came Adney's most pathetic attempt to sell the models. By this time, Minnie had lost her sight and was in need of constant care. Contacting the president of the Montreal Association for the Blind, Adney proposed that McGill might be prepared to acquire the model canoe collection by making a donation of $5,000 to the Association, in return for which the Association might look after Minnie. The proposal was declined without comment, and the Adneys left Montreal for Woodstock, where Adney would reside for the rest of his life.

In a surprisingly intimate letter to Lionel Judah several years later, Adney described conditions in Woodstock. He and Minnie had moved into Adney's rural bungalow, which had been unoccupied for some time, its roof falling in and its floor rotting away.

> It is an indescribable relief which I did not realize until I arrived here from the strain of the past couple of years. It is a wonderful place, a mingling of old orchard trees, and now great timber spruce and a bungalo which needed an infinite number of repairs.

The Adneys had no electricity, running water or toilet. Minnie had the only bedroom while Adney lived in a small storage shed at the rear of the house. The couple had arrived in Woodstock with $45, part of it supplied by the Montreal Family Welfare Society and part by the Association for the Blind. Now, after a long but prickly marriage, he had a wife who was entirely dependent upon him. Yet somehow under these trying conditions, when Tappan Adney was not shoveling his long lane and cutting firewood for a house that "leaked like a sieve," he managed to continue his research and model building.

Lionel Judah continued to keep in touch with Adney's great friend at Woodstock, Dr. George F. Clarke. In 1934, when Clarke wrote Judah that Adney was so poor that he was smoking red willow bark, Judah sent him a large package of his favorite tobacco for Christmas. It is possible that the Adney–Judah "feud" was in fact a one-sided affair fueled by Adney's irascible nature. Without a doubt, his relationship with Judah was colored by what

his son, Glenn, called Adney's "inability to get along peaceably with his fellow men."

In 1937 Minnie died, and in 1939 McGill entered negotiations with Adney to clear his $1,000 loan through the purchase of his model collection with money from private donors. Adney later commented: "McGill did make me an offer, which amounted to about a third of its admitted valuation, and in a form that I could not well accept."

THE MARINERS' MUSEUM

From Minnie's death onward, Adney lived alone, surrounded by his vast collection of research notes, his model-building materials and his recent models that had not gone to McGill. These were the conditions in which Nola and Fred Hill found him. Frederick F. Hill was a field representative for the recently established Mariners'

Lionel Judah, curator of the McGill University museums, standing behind a 22½ foot Têtes de Boule canoe built by Quayshish of Manouan, Quebec, in 1929 for trader William Mitledge. Mitledge and Quayshish's son, Michael, used this canoe to shoot the dangerous Steamboat Channel of the Lachine Rapids at Montreal.

Museum in Newport News, Virginia. While visiting the McGill Ethnology Museum, the Hills saw a group of Native bark canoes, as Nola Hill stated in her memoir *Museum Pieces*, "stacked carelessly on top of each other, covered with a heavy accumulation of dust and apparently given little attention." The museum could not offer much information about Adney, so the Hills initiated their own search. Nola wrote:

> We went after him with all the tenacity of a ferret seeking food in a hidden retreat. Telephone books gave no clues. Old issues in the library, however, gave his name and address ... We felt like Scotland Yard officers must feel when they approach their object of search.

They found Adney surrounded by his homemade furniture and a few possessions he had rescued from Montreal creditors. One small room was packed with birchbark, spruce roots, and willow and ash cuttings.

The Hills approached Adney about the possible sale of his model collection to the Mariners' Museum and, after much correspondence and discussions with Glenn, an offer was made in January 1940. Adney accepted. The agreement called for the Mariners' to pay off Adney's McGill loan and take posession of the entire model collection at McGill and in his bungalow. Adney was to be paid $100 per month so that he could continue work on his canoe manuscript. Nola Hill commented, "I was not without misgivings that the [Mariners'] Museum paid off the loan of $1000.00 and took a very fine collection from the country where it rightfully belonged."

When Adney informed Diamond Jenness of the sale, Jenness replied:

> It is a shame that your model canoes cannot stay in Canada. I would give a good deal to be allowed to purchase them for our museum here [the National Museum of Canada], but we operate on a shoestring ... Some day, when it is too late perhaps, the Canadian people will wake up and decide they want a real museum in the capital city.

At the time the models were sold, Adney valued them at about $30,000. As part of the agreement, the Mariners' Museum paid off the McGill loan in the amount of $1,450 ($1,000 plus $450 interest) and gave $1,000 to Glenn Adney, probably money that Glenn had lent his father over the years. The museum also paid some of Adney's personal expenses, such as repairs to the

Woodstock house, and apparently paid Adney $15,000, part in cash and part in the form of the monthly stipend of $100 for an indefinite period, during which Adney would write his long-planned book. Some details of the transaction are unclear; for instance, Adney's note on the matter does not indicate whether the $15,000 included the loan from McGill and the payment to Glenn, or was in addition to these payments. Adney commented separately that the $100 monthly stipend was part of what was owed him for the models, the remaining cash settlement being agreed upon to make it appear to Mariners' trustees that the museum had struck a good deal.

In an intriguing sidelight, letters in the McCord Museum at McGill indicate that McGill attempted to block the sale to the Mariners' Museum, claiming ownership of the models because Adney had not repaid his loan in the time stipulated. An attorney assured Adney, however, that no court would bar the sale. Once again, Adney blamed Judah, accusing him of urging McGill's new Principal, Cyril James, to assert that Adney had legally forfeited the models. According to Adney, James in fact had offered to buy the collection from him "for whatever the Mariners' Museum was proposing to do."

With the models purchased, the Hills were left with one major frustration. Adney's monthly stipend was supposed to support him while he wrote his book, but whenever he got money he soon gave much of it away to his Native friends. In 1947, the Hills suspended Adney's payments, reporting to the Mariners' Museum that Adney had done no work on the book in the preceding year. The book project remained unfinished as Adney became increasingly involved in Native advocacy and began work on two other books, one on Native issues with the New Brunswick government and the other a Maliseet dictionary. As Adney considered the $100 monthly payment part of his compensation for the models, he felt no pressure to produce the book. The Hills visited him once or twice a year to buy him clothes and keep him in groceries. They also had electricity brought to the bungalow and replaced the typewriter that Adney had carried over the Chilkoot Pass and had continued to use until some of the letters were worn off the keys.

After his models arrived safely at the Mariners' Museum, Adney was invited to visit and check the information that accompanied them. The Hills picked him up at Grand Central Station in New York for the trip to Virginia. Nola Hill described Adney, now in his 70s, in his travel ensemble:

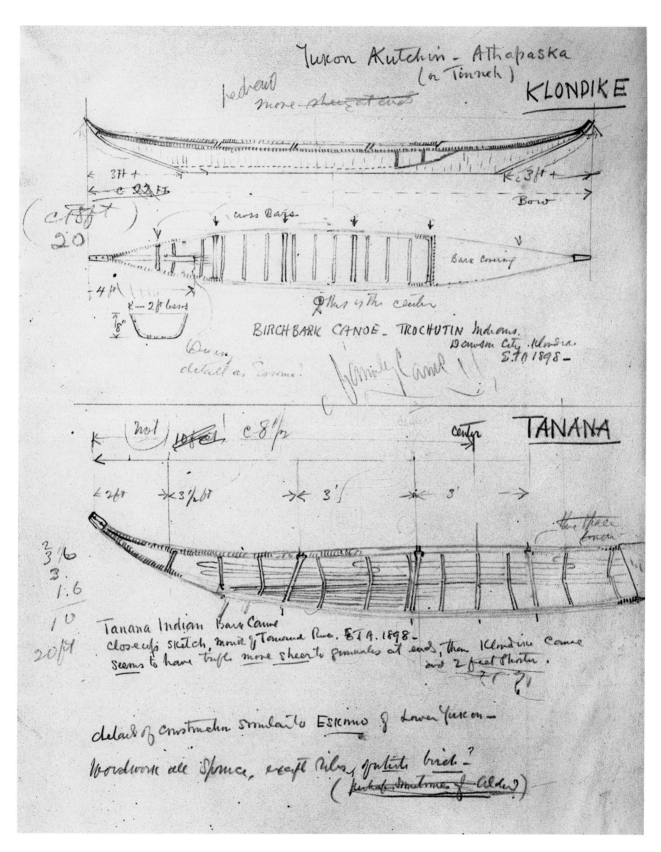

As early as 1898 Adney was making detailed sketches of Native craft while in the
Klondike. These sketches relate to models #63 (p. 94) and #86 (p. 95).

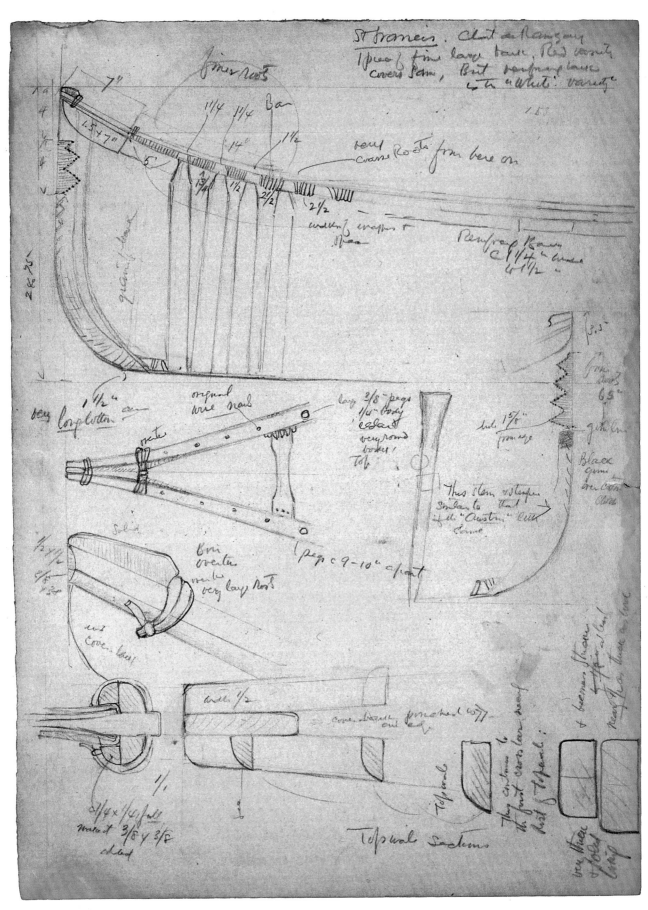

Detailed drawings for the building of one of his St. Francis Abenaki models, based on Native models at the Chateau de Ramezay Museum in Montreal (#52, p. 52, or #103, p. 52).

A man over six feet tall, erect and military in stature ... He stepped from the train wearing a coonskin cap several sizes too small ... The front of his well ventilated overcoat, green with age, featured the markings of the proverbial forty-seven varieties of soups, and was buttoned out of line. Where a button or two were missing, shiny nails served the purpose. Overshoes ... flopped noisily on the station floor.

In June 1949, shortly before Adney died, he wrote to Glenn to impress upon him the value of his manuscript material and said he was leaving in Glenn's hands the disposal of the material. After Adney died, Glenn gave the manuscript to the Mariners' Museum, which in turn passed on the linguistic material to Peabody Essex. Glenn gave his father's Klondike material to the famous Arctic explorer Vilhjalmur Stefansson, who in turn presented it to Dartmouth College in Hanover, New Hampshire. In the end, the Mariners' Museum had obtained not only the world's foremost collection of North American Native canoe models, but also the world's foremost research collection on the continent's Native canoe cultures. Without Adney's monumental corpus of research and the canoe models that so closely complemented it, our knowledge of Native and fur trade cultures would be vastly diminished.

Tappan Adney died in 1950 at the age of 82, in his Woodstock bungalow, surrounded by his beloved birds and squirrels, his lifetime of research notes and drawings, and a few of his remaining treasured models. By all accounts he could be obstinate and opinionated, but never self-important. Seemingly oblivious to his meager surroundings and, as Nola Hill remarked, to the end of his life as "rugged as an old pine knot," Adney had single-handedly assured that the great heritage of the bark canoe would not die.

After Adney's death, his unfinished manuscript, notes and drawings were transformed by Howard Chapelle of the Smithsonian Institution into *The Bark Canoes and Skin Boats of North America*, published in 1964. Anyone who has worked with the Adney papers at the Mariners' Museum will have a great appreciation of the overwhelming task Chapelle undertook in making sense of this chaotic, but extraordinarily rich, collection. Adney intended to write about only the Native bark canoes of the continent; Chapelle decided to add his own section on the skin craft of the Inuit. It was a good decision. The book continues to this day to be the bible of canoe and kayak scholars and builders.

A painting by Edwin B. Child in 1901 of Adney as he was in the Klondike working as an artist and correspondent for *Harper's Weekly* and the *London Chronicle* in 1897–98.

Canoe Models

East Coast 28

Eastern Woodlands 50

Northwest 84

Asia and South America 104

Fur Trade 120

Canoe Model Details 128

CANOES OF THE
East Coast

The birchbark canoes of the East Coast region, especially those of the Maliseet, were regarded by Adney as being the most advanced in the world. This region, from Newfoundland to Maine, produced some of the best birchbark on the continent.

The Native groups of this region are the Mi'kmaq, the Maliseet, the Passamaquoddy and the now extinct Beothuk of Newfoundland. The Abenaki of Maine are considered later in this book, in the discussion of the eastern woodlands tradition.

The Mi'kmaq traditionally inhabited Nova Scotia, Prince Edward Island, the Gaspé region of Quebec, and New Brunswick from the north shore to the Bay of Fundy. The Maliseet and Passamaquoddy (a branch of the Maliseet) were centered on the Saint John and St. Croix Rivers, Passamaquoddy Bay at the mouth of the St. Croix, and (in early days) along the Penobscot and Kennebec Rivers. The Beothuk inhabited Newfoundland, migrating annually between coastal fishing and the inland caribou hunt. Because none of the Beothuk survived the European advance into their territory, their canoes will probably always retain an element of mystery.

Bay of Chaleur Mi'kmaq Birchbark Ocean Canoe

Based on a canoe in the collection of the Canadian Museum of Civilization, collected in 1913. Adney saw similar canoes at Burnt Church, New Brunswick. Adney built this model in 1928, based on old style Mi'kmaq construction, except for the use of nails on the gunwale cap. Nails were introduced into east coast Native building in the second half of the nineteenth century. The fender along the side of the canoe, designed to protect the canoe from bumps and the scraping of paddles, is unusual. The floorboards are held in by split ash ribs. Sailing became common among east coast Native groups after contact with Europeans. The Mi'kmaq usually used a simple square sail with a diagonal pole, but this canoe has a sprit sail. The mast is secured by a thwart nailed across the gunwale caps and the heel is stepped into a block.

MM #**84**   L: 51"   W: 8"   D: 5⅜"

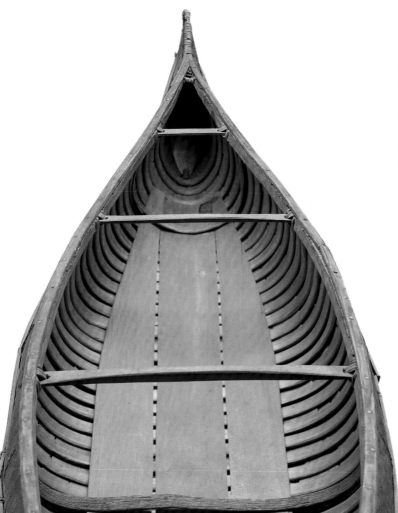

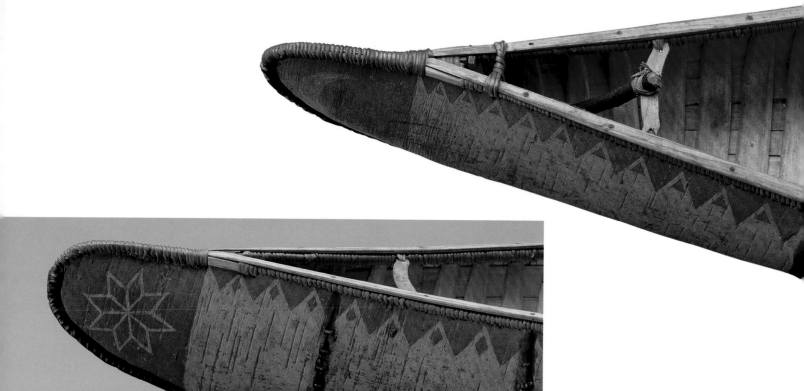

Mi'kmaq Birchbark Woods Canoe

Based on canoes built in the region of Bear River, Nova Scotia. Adney built this model in 1933 in the old Mi'kmaq style. The gunwale caps are pegged rather than nailed, and continuous lashing is clearly visible around the single gunwale. The salmon spear represents the foremost occupation of the Mi'kmaq. The decorations, produced by scraping away the darker outer layer of bark to reveal the lighter inner bark, are typical. The stick lashed to the bow thwart is either part of a mast structure or intended as a handle to aid in carrying the craft (see Maliseet #64, p. 36).

MM #**101** L: 36" W: 6" D: 3"

30

TOP: **Mi'kmaq Birchbark Woods Canoe**

Based on an original Mi'kmaq canoe at Weymouth, Nova Scotia. Adney built this model in 1926. It represents the era after 1890 when the Mi'kmaq began to build canoes using nails. The thwarts are notched into the inwale and the gunwale cap is nailed to the gunwale. The eight-pointed star is based on a Mi'kmaq sketch from Bear River, Nova Scotia, and on Mi'kmaq models in the McCord Museum, Montreal.

MM #**90** L: 34" W: 6⅜" D: 4"

MIDDLE: **Mi'kmaq Birchbark Woods Canoe**

Based on Mi'kmaq canoes built at Bear River, Nova Scotia. The "camp" decoration (the zigzag pattern representing a series of teepees) along the gunwale is a typical Mi'kmaq design. The crescent moon is the private mark of builder Joseph Pictou (Picto).

MM #**148** L: 35" W: 6⅜" D: 4"

BOTTOM: **Restigouche River Mi'kmaq Birchbark Canoe**

Based generally on large Bay of Chaleur old-style sea-going canoes, and specifically on a large Mi'kmaq model in the American Museum of Natural History in New York, dated 1890. This model is the only Mi'kmaq example Adney could find of the old method of pegging gunwale caps. Adney built this model in 1926. For a canoe of this size, it was necessary to add a second piece of bark amidships.

MM #**124** L: 44" W: 8" D: 5³⁄₁₆"

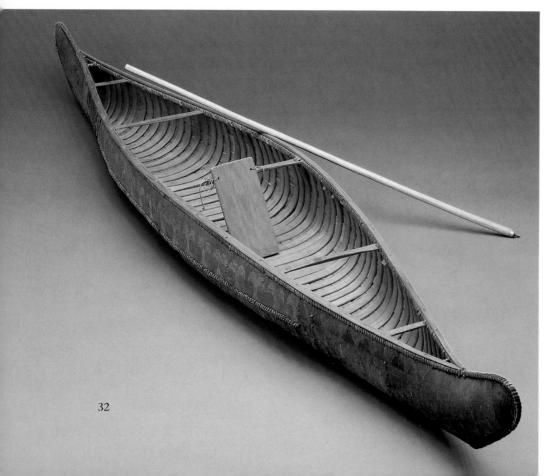

Mi'kmaq Restigouche Rough Water Birchbark Canoe

Based on a Mi'kmaq canoe at the Canadian Museum of Civilization from Bathurst, New Brunswick. Adney built this model in 1926 in the ancient traditional manner, with a pegged gunwale cap and the narrow profile of earlier Mi'kmaq canoes. The rather flimsy-looking ends were stuffed with moss and cedar shavings, which added strength and helped maintain their shape. The rise of the gunwale amidships is typical of the sea-going Mi'kmaq canoe. The Restigouche, one of the great salmon rivers of North America, is shallow, and the spiked pole was used for poling upriver. The cedar board is a back-rest for a passenger.

MM #**135** L: 51" W: 8" D: 5"

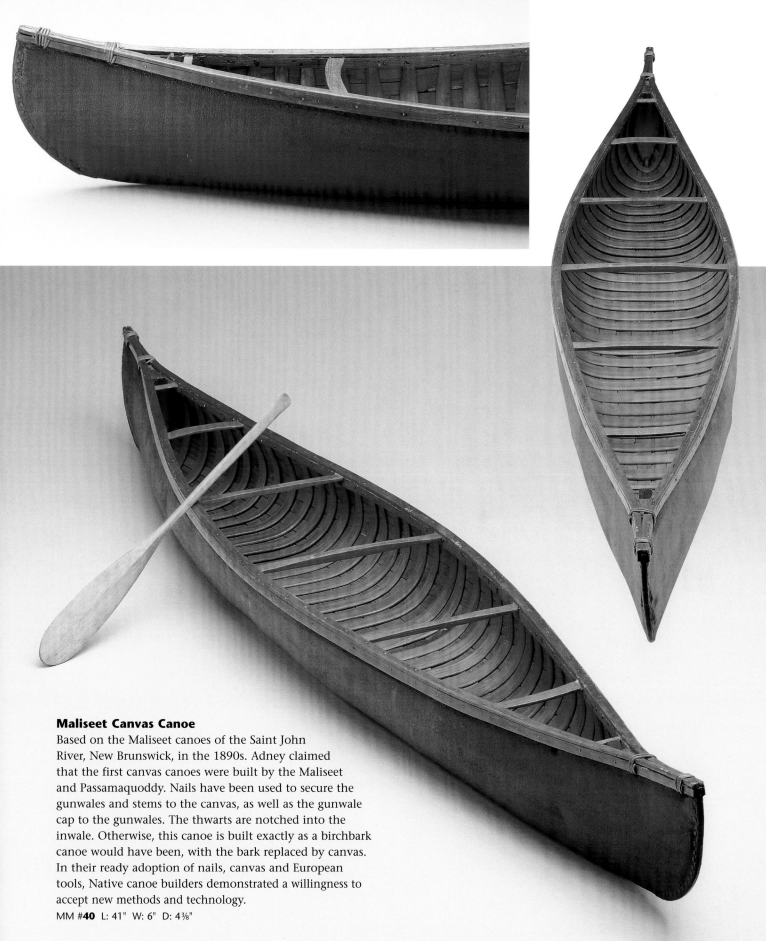

Maliseet Canvas Canoe

Based on the Maliseet canoes of the Saint John
River, New Brunswick, in the 1890s. Adney claimed
that the first canvas canoes were built by the Maliseet
and Passamaquoddy. Nails have been used to secure the
gunwales and stems to the canvas, as well as the gunwale
cap to the gunwales. The thwarts are notched into the
inwale. Otherwise, this canoe is built exactly as a birchbark
canoe would have been, with the bark replaced by canvas.
In their ready adoption of nails, canvas and European
tools, Native canoe builders demonstrated a willingness to
accept new methods and technology.

MM #**40** L: 41" W: 6" D: 4⅜"

TOP: Maliseet Birchbark Canoe
Based on a Saint John River canoe built by Frank Sacobie, Lower River, New Brunswick, in 1918. This is a good example of what Adney called the "decadence" that had overtaken Maliseet canoe building by the twentieth century. Roofing asphalt has replaced pitch and the side bark has been fastened with carpet tacks. Blunt ends have superseded the elegant lines of earlier Maliseet canoes.
MM #**39** L: 40" W: 7⅛" D: 5"

BOTTOM: Maliseet Birchbark River Canoe
Based on a Maliseet canoe built at Denys Point (Princeton, Maine) by Tomah Josephs in the mid-1890s and on the interior features of an 1873 canoe from Eastport, Maine, now at the Peabody Museum, Harvard. Adney was meticulous about details, so it is clear that Maliseet builders were using nails by 1873.
MM #**61** L: 38" W: 7" D: 5"

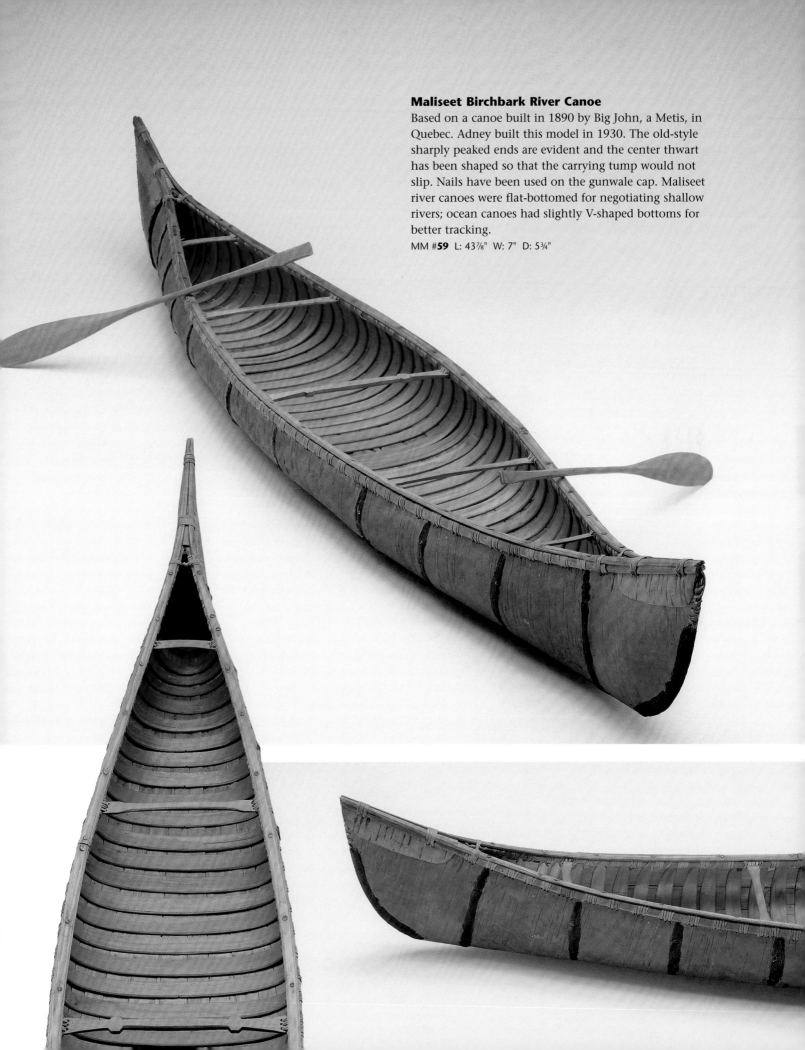

Maliseet Birchbark River Canoe
Based on a canoe built in 1890 by Big John, a Metis, in Quebec. Adney built this model in 1930. The old-style sharply peaked ends are evident and the center thwart has been shaped so that the carrying tump would not slip. Nails have been used on the gunwale cap. Maliseet river canoes were flat-bottomed for negotiating shallow rivers; ocean canoes had slightly V-shaped bottoms for better tracking.

MM #**59** L: 43⅞" W: 7" D: 5¾"

Maliseet Two-and-a-Half-Fathom Birchbark River Canoe

Based on the Maliseet canoes of the Saint John River. The decoration is typical of the Tobique River region in the 1880s. The beaver and leaf design on the wulegessis (the flap of bark visible in the bottom right photograph, that protects the gunwale end lashings) was the private mark (dupskodegun) of John Solis of Tobique. The eight-pointed star was a common Maliseet symbol, as were the hoops (earrings) and zigzag shapes along the gunwale. The fiddlehead design below the mid-gunwale was a good-luck symbol. Adney built this model in 1926. The gunwale caps are pegged in the old fashion, and the stem protrudes — an unusual feature in Maliseet canoes. The two paddles have shafts that are progressively narrowed, a feature unique to East Coast paddles. Adney called the stick lashed to the end thwart an ancient carrying apparatus, shown to him by Peter Bear.

MM #**64** L: 34" W: 7" D: 4⅞"

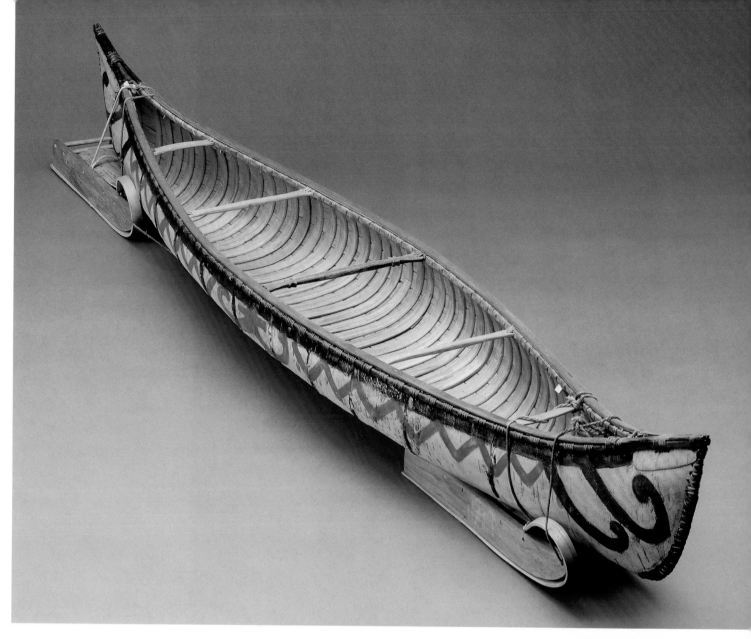

Maliseet River Canoe

Based on a Saint John River Maliseet model
dating from the 1830s, given to Adney
by the estate of Colonel Herbert Dibble of
Woodstock. The spiral fiddlehead decoration
is painted on the bark, as is the camp zigzag
pattern. The Maliseet boiled alder bark to
obtain the red pigment used on their canoes.
The firesteel, a fiddlehead joined at the center
by a cross, was a common Maliseet design.

During the spring breakup of the rivers,
the Maliseet used sleds to pull their canoes
to open water for the muskrat hunt — a
practice that continued until the end of the
nineteenth century.

MM #**150**   L: 42"   W: 6⅞"   D: 6"

TOP: **Maliseet Birchbark Canoe**
Based on a pre-Confederation (1867) Native model of a Lower St. Lawrence River Maliseet canoe that Adney found at the Château de Ramezay Museum in Montreal, Quebec. Adding the side panels of bark in two stages made the panels easier to sew.
MM #**69** L: 38" W: 8⅜" D: 5"

BOTTOM: **Maliseet Birchbark Racing Canoe**
Based on a Maliseet canoe built on the Saint John River in 1888 for a European client. Nails have been used, but the decorations on the bark are traditional. The long, sleek lines of this canoe would have made it very fast. Both the Maliseet and Mi'kmaq had strong racing traditions reaching back long before the arrival of Europeans. Racing canoes usually had a V-shaped bottom for better tracking.
MM #**154** L: 46" W: 6" D: 4"

Maliseet Birchbark Canoe with Shoes

Based on a Saint John River canoe built by Adney's mentor, Peter Jo, in 1890, the year that Adney built his first canoe. His name can be seen on the wulegessis, the flap of bark that protects the gunwale end lashing. The cedar "shoes" were used to protect the bottom of the canoe when it was being dragged up shallow rivers to avoid portages. To keep the shoes from slipping, rawhide lashings attached the shoes at bow and stern and split ash attached them to the thwarts. Shown with the model are a fishing spear and an unusually fine paddle, with the traditional long, rectangular Maliseet grip.

MM #**67**   L: 46"   W: 7"   D: 5"

Maliseet Spruce Bark Canoe

Based on a model by Peter Bear of Tobique, New Brunswick, the last of the Maliseet spruce bark canoe builders. Built in 1895, the original model is part of the Adney collection at the Mariners' Museum. Peter Bear made the ends watertight by pushing spruce or fir buds, "chewed up fine," into the cracks. Clay was also used for this purpose.

Adney built this model in 1931, using black spruce from Quebec. The inside gunwales are alder and the outside white birch. This type of canoe was for temporary use and thus was fashioned quickly and crudely. There was only one thwart, usually a willow branch, which was shaved at the ends, looped around the gunwale, and wrapped back around itself. The two other crossbars consisted of cedar bark looped over the gunwales and, like the center thwart, wrapped around itself.

MM #**121** L: 36" W: 8" D: 5"

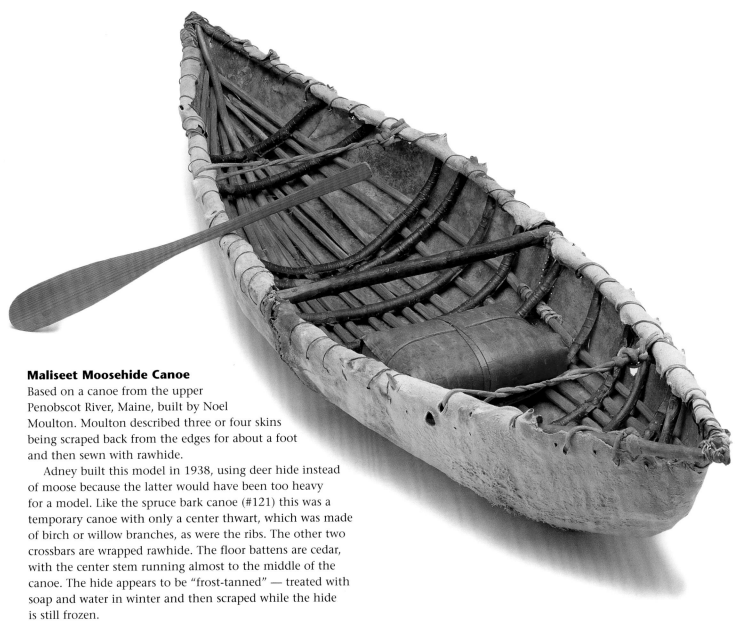

Maliseet Moosehide Canoe

Based on a canoe from the upper
Penobscot River, Maine, built by Noel
Moulton. Moulton described three or four skins
being scraped back from the edges for about a foot
and then sewn with rawhide.

Adney built this model in 1938, using deer hide instead
of moose because the latter would have been too heavy
for a model. Like the spruce bark canoe (#121) this was a
temporary canoe with only a center thwart, which was made
of birch or willow branches, as were the ribs. The other two
crossbars are wrapped rawhide. The floor battens are cedar,
with the center stem running almost to the middle of the
canoe. The hide appears to be "frost-tanned" — treated with
soap and water in winter and then scraped while the hide
is still frozen.

MM #**140** L: 32" W: 10⅛" D: 6⅛"

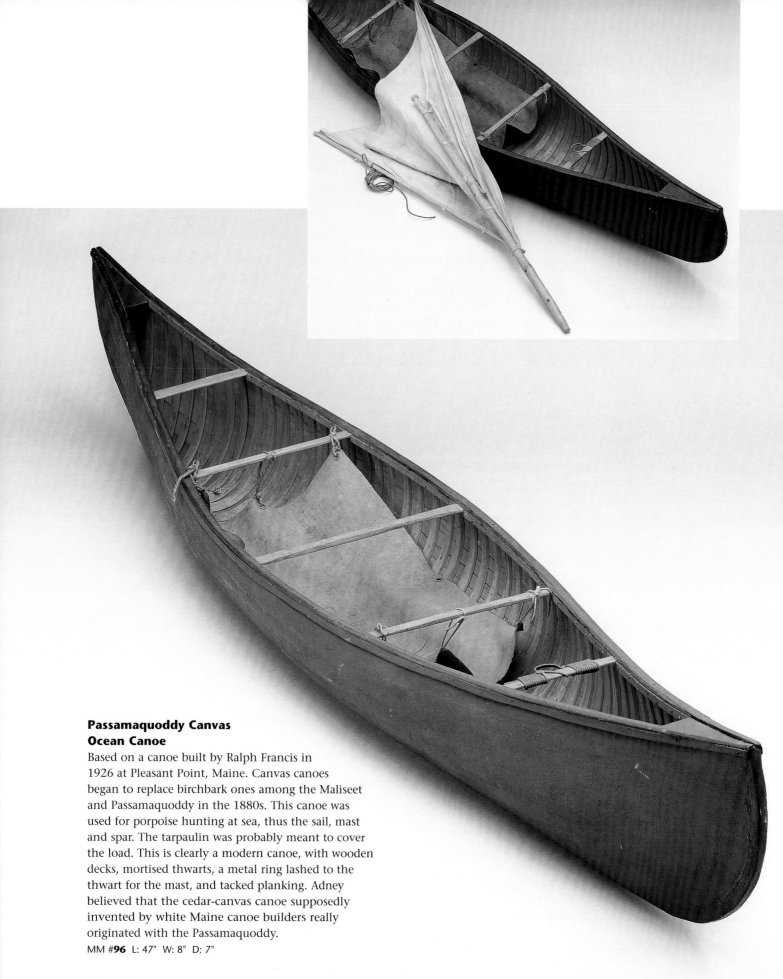

**Passamaquoddy Canvas
Ocean Canoe**

Based on a canoe built by Ralph Francis in
1926 at Pleasant Point, Maine. Canvas canoes
began to replace birchbark ones among the Maliseet
and Passamaquoddy in the 1880s. This canoe was
used for porpoise hunting at sea, thus the sail, mast
and spar. The tarpaulin was probably meant to cover
the load. This is clearly a modern canoe, with wooden
decks, mortised thwarts, a metal ring lashed to the
thwart for the mast, and tacked planking. Adney
believed that the cedar-canvas canoe supposedly
invented by white Maine canoe builders really
originated with the Passamaquoddy.
MM #**96** L: 47" W: 8" D: 7"

Passamaquoddy Birchbark River Canoe
Based on a canoe collected by G.A. Peabody at Eastport, Maine, in 1878 and donated to the Peabody Museum, Harvard University. The old-style pointed bow is evident, as is the old-style cross-stitching at the bow. The tumpline notch on the center thwart is clear. The paddle is made of cedar. The top photograph shows especially well the narrowing of the canoe's ends, which gave the Maliseet and Passamaquoddy craft such distinctive elegance.

MM #**117** L: 41⅝" W: 6⅞" D: 6⅜"

Passamaquoddy Painted Birchbark Canoe

Based on a Passamaquoddy model built in 1897. The original canoe was used for hunting porpoise and seal and had a slightly V-shaped hull to suit it for open water. This shape was created by bending the ribs sharply at the center and inserting a narrow strake of sheathing along the centerline. Both the exterior and interior are painted. An eagle is painted on the bow and the words "Frenchman's Bay" appear on the stern.

MM #**46** L: 38" W: 7" D: 4"

Passamaquoddy Birchbark Ocean Canoe

Representing an ancient Passamaquoddy design for ocean hunting, especially for porpoise, this model was specifically based on an 1873 canoe from Eastport, Maine; an 1849 model made by Soisin Denis, and another dated 1798. All three are now located at the Peabody Museum, Harvard University. Adney built this model in 1927. It is deeper than it is wide, an unusual feature. The canoe would have carried a considerable load, and until it was loaded it probably would have been unstable on ocean swells.

MM #**126** L: 50" W: 8" D: 9"

Beothuk Birchbark Canoe

Adney was fascinated by Beothuk canoes. The dearth of historical information about Beothuk canoes has given rise to much speculation by canoe builders and scholars about the unique and odd shape of these craft. Their basic shape is known from early descriptions and a scattering of models, but construction details are not known. Citing evidence based on linguistics and gunwale construction, Adney believed that the Beothuk were related to the Maliseet rather than to the Mi'kmaq. He speculated that they had originally been a mainland people who, at some ancient time, had been pushed out of their territory as the Mi'kmaq migrated south from the region of the Cree and Montagnais. Mi'kmaq canoes are undeniably similar in construction to those of the Cree and Montagnais.

MM #**95** L: 34" W: 9" D: 7"

Beothuk Birchbark Canoe

Adney built a number of Beothuk models. Two are at the Canadian Museum of Civilization, together with notes on their differences. In 1767 Lieutenant John Cartwright wrote of a Beothuk canoe with a gunwale made of two pieces that met in a V at the center and were lashed together. When Adney attempted this construction, however, he decided that it was impossible. The backbone of a bark canoe consists of its gunwales, and only a continuous arched gunwale would have the strength to survive ocean swells. Extant models offer no clues as to how the gunwales were constructed or lashed. The very high ends had no clear purpose, except, perhaps, for shelter when the canoe was overturned.

MM #**45** L: 42" W: 12" D: 8⅜"

Beothuk Birchbark Canoe

It is thought that the Beothuk had two basic types of canoe: a sea-going version and another type for interior rivers. This model represents the sea-going type, with the V-shaped hull and straight bottom creating a keel. The Beothuk are known to have made voyages of up to 60 miles across open ocean; some sea-going canoes were over 20 feet long. The extreme rise midships would have helped deflect waves and also would have allowed the canoe to be heeled over (Adney claimed to 35 degrees) while a porpoise or other large catch was hauled in at the quarter; rocks may have been used for ballast. Sticks at the bow and stern were used to pull the canoe ashore and also to provide more head room when the canoe was used for shelter. The ribs and sheathing are spruce, as Newfoundland lacks cedar trees.

MM #**138** L: 37" W: 9" D: 9⅛"

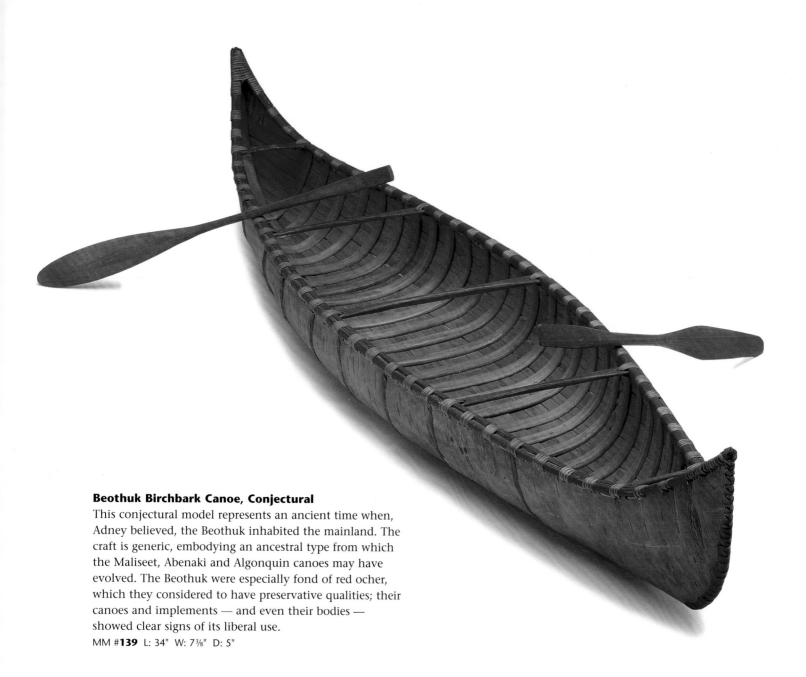

Beothuk Birchbark Canoe, Conjectural

This conjectural model represents an ancient time when, Adney believed, the Beothuk inhabited the mainland. The craft is generic, embodying an ancestral type from which the Maliseet, Abenaki and Algonquin canoes may have evolved. The Beothuk were especially fond of red ocher, which they considered to have preservative qualities; their canoes and implements — and even their bodies — showed clear signs of its liberal use.

MM #**139** L: 34" W: 7⅜" D: 5"

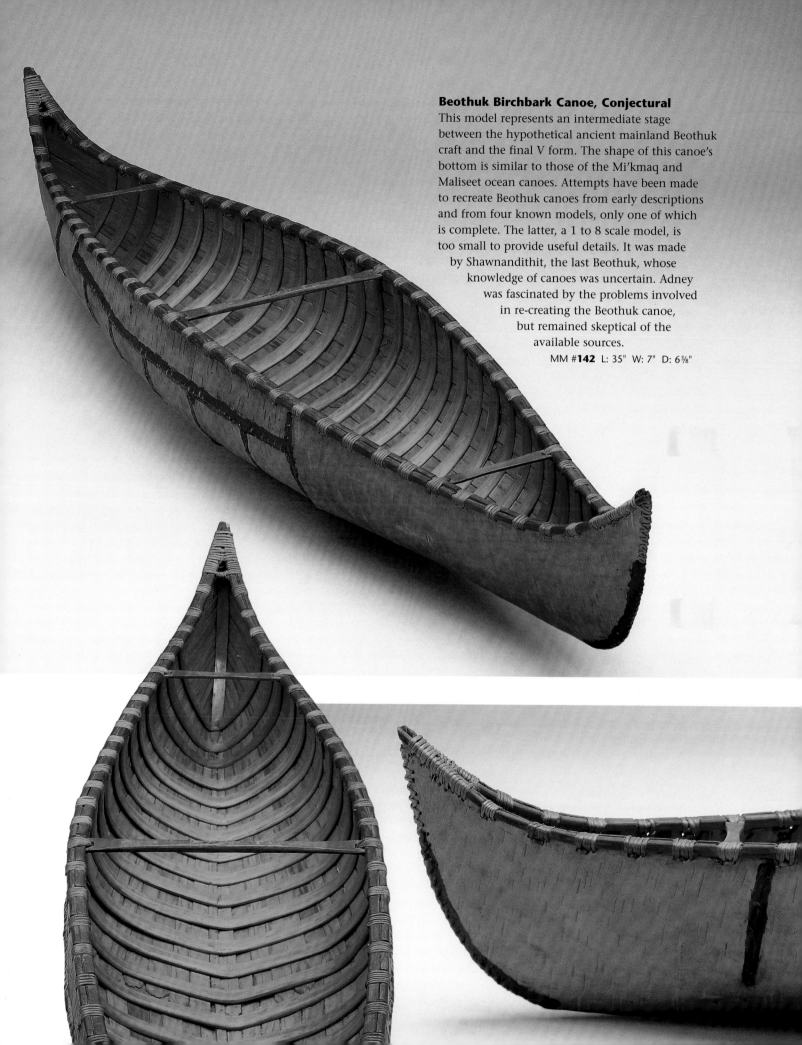

Beothuk Birchbark Canoe, Conjectural

This model represents an intermediate stage between the hypothetical ancient mainland Beothuk craft and the final V form. The shape of this canoe's bottom is similar to those of the Mi'kmaq and Maliseet ocean canoes. Attempts have been made to recreate Beothuk canoes from early descriptions and from four known models, only one of which is complete. The latter, a 1 to 8 scale model, is too small to provide useful details. It was made by Shawnandithit, the last Beothuk, whose knowledge of canoes was uncertain. Adney was fascinated by the problems involved in re-creating the Beothuk canoe, but remained skeptical of the available sources.

MM #**142** L: 35" W: 7" D: 6⅜"

Canoes of the
Eastern Woodlands

The Eastern Woodlands, in canoe terms, is a vast region which stretches from the coast of Labrador and Quebec in the east to Saskatchewan in the west, and from the northern territory adjoining Inuit lands in Quebec, Ontario and Manitoba down to northern Maine, New York State, Michigan, Wisconsin and Minnesota in the south. This region contained a great variety of peoples — from the Eastern and Western Cree of the North, and the Eastern Cree's close relations, the Naskapi and Montagnais (collectively known as the Innu), to the Algonquins and Têtes de Boule of the St. Lawrence and Ottawa Rivers. Farther to the west were the Ojibwa, known in Manitoba as the Saulteaux and in American territory as the Chippewa. The region was also home to migrant peoples, the Iroquois in the Montreal area and the St. Francis Abenaki in the St. Lawrence Valley, who both became important canoe builders for the fur trade. The St. Francis Abenaki were composed of groups of Maliseet, Kennebec and Penobscot who had been driven from their homes in New England and migrated north.

Although Adney's favorite canoe was always the Maliseet, the central theme of his work was that the Native canoes of the St. Lawrence–Ottawa River–Great Lakes axis (those of the Abenaki, Algonquin, Têtes de Boule and Ojibwa) were transformed into the voyaging canoes of the Europeans. Adney held that this historical process was unique in the history of the world, and could happen only where the world's most generous system of waterways and the bark of the birch tree came together.

St. Francis Abenaki Birchbark Canoe

Based on a canoe built by Nicola Panadis, Pierreville, Quebec, in 1895. Adney built this model in 1930. It is a good example of double gunwales, group lashing and pegged gunwale caps. The canoe has an unusual scalloped gunwale reinforcing strip. The gunwales are cedar, the ribs spruce and the thwarts jack pine. Each builder had his own way of measuring. Panadis, the last of the St. Francis builders, measured not in feet and inches, but in the length of his arms and the width of his hands and fingers. Adney carefully recorded Panadis' measurements, but remarked that he had "inexcusably neglected to measure old Panadis himself."

The St. Francis Abenaki were composed of elements of the Maliseet, Kennebec and Penobscot who had been driven from their homes in New England and migrated north to the St. Lawrence, where they settled between Montreal and Quebec City and became firm allies of the French.

MM #**113** L: 34" W: 7⅛" D: 6⁵⁄₁₆"

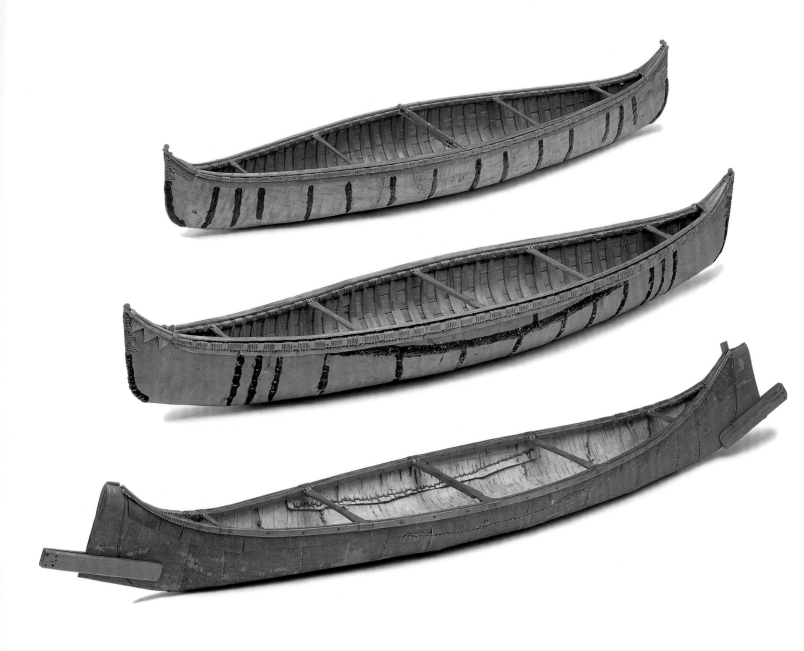

TOP: St. Francis Abenaki Birchbark Canoe

Based on an 1865 Abenaki model, now in the Château de Ramezay, Montreal, and on a canoe built for Mr. A. Austin, Chambly, Quebec, in 1865. Adney built this model in 1929. The reinforced center thwart is for portaging. It distributes the weight along the gunwale and lessens the springiness of the thwart while portaging. The protruding stempiece is unusual.

MM #**52** L: 25" W: 5⅝" D: 4"

MIDDLE: St. Francis Abenaki Birchbark Canoe

Based on a canoe built in 1866 at Becancoeur, Quebec, and now in the Château de Ramezay, Montreal. Adney built this model in 1927. The canoe is a larger version of #52. The Native people who left New England after King Philip's War of 1675 and came north to the St. Lawrence were given a land grant at Becancoeur by the French Crown.

MM #**103** L: 33" W: 7⅛" D: 6"

BOTTOM: St. Francis Abenaki Two-and-a-Half-Fathom Birchbark Canoe

Based on a canoe built by Nicola Panadis, Pierreville, Quebec, in 1900. This model represents the fifth stage of canoe building, just after the canoe has been lifted from the building bed. The inner seams and gores will be pitched with a softer pitch than is used on the exterior; it should push through to the outside.

MM #**122** L: 43" W: 8" D: 6⅜"

Modified Abenaki Birchbark Canoe

Based on a canoe built by an Algonquin builder, Antoine Michel, Chief of the Maniwaki Algonquin, from a photograph by F.W. Waugh, 1916, at the Canadian Museum of Civilization. Adney built this model in 1926. The three temporary thwarts were used for portaging and occasionally for sitting on while paddling, to ease cramped knees. For both purposes, they took the strain off the mortising of the thwarts.

Maniwaki has long been known for its canoe building. Today, it is the foremost Native canoe-building center in North America.

MM #**97** L: 36" W: 6⅞" D: 5⅜"

Abenaki Birchbark Canoe

Based on a canoe built by Algonquin builders
Amab and Tommy Sarazin, Golden Lake, Ontario,
in 1927. Adney built this model in 1927. The
model is somewhat rough and the ends blunt.
Altogether, this is not an elegant model. The
Sarazin canoe-building dynasty of Golden Lake
and Maniwaki had a reputation for building some
of the best canoes of the era. This model perhaps
does not do justice to the original.

MM #**108**   L: 30"   W: 6⅞"   D: 4"

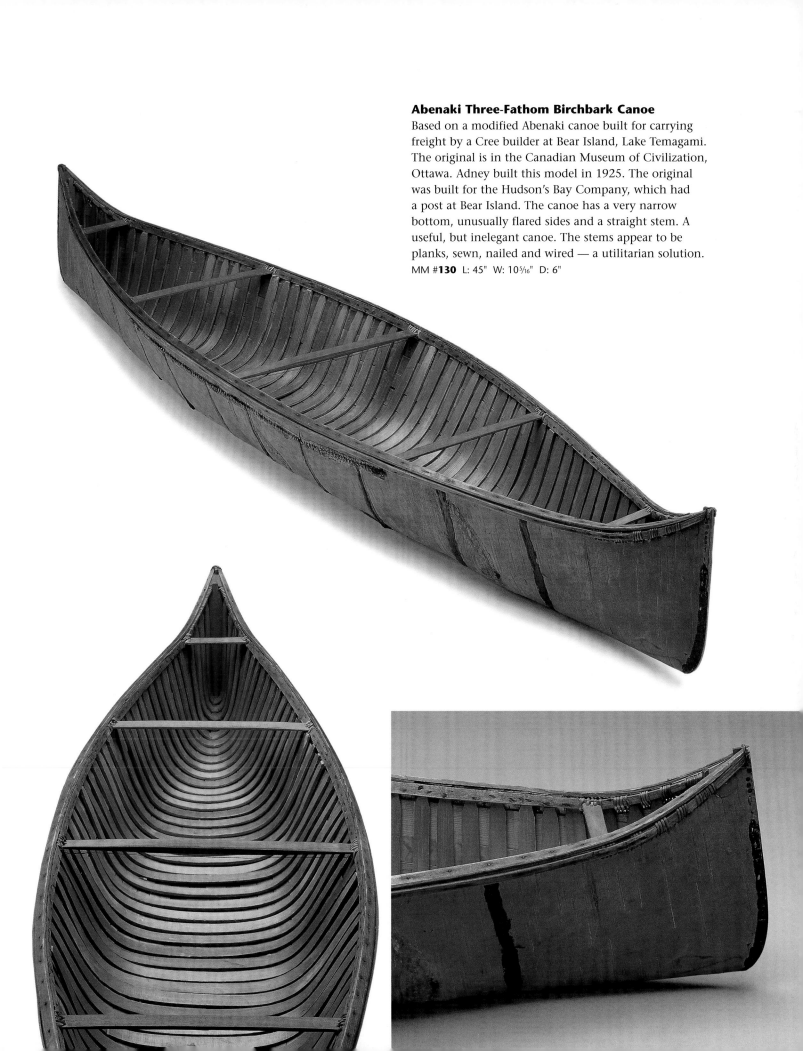

Abenaki Three-Fathom Birchbark Canoe

Based on a modified Abenaki canoe built for carrying freight by a Cree builder at Bear Island, Lake Temagami. The original is in the Canadian Museum of Civilization, Ottawa. Adney built this model in 1925. The original was built for the Hudson's Bay Company, which had a post at Bear Island. The canoe has a very narrow bottom, unusually flared sides and a straight stem. A useful, but inelegant canoe. The stems appear to be planks, sewn, nailed and wired — a utilitarian solution.

MM #**130** L: 45" W: 10⁵⁄₁₆" D: 6"

TOP: Abenaki Birchbark Canoe

Based on a canoe built by Peter White Duck of Oka, Quebec, in about 1887, and now in the McCord Museum, Montreal. Adney built this model in 1929. At the ends, the bark has been trimmed and sewn through the plank stems. The gunwale caps have been pegged (the pegs can be seen protruding under the inner gunwale).

MM #**106** L: 31" W: 7" D: 4"

BOTTOM: Algonquin Eastern Abenaki-Type Birchbark Canoe

Based on a canoe built at Maniwaki, Quebec, on the Gatineau River, and now in the McCord Museum, Montreal. Adney built this model in 1926. The protruding stems were typical of the St. Francis builders; the three temporary thwarts were for distributing the weight while portaging and for sitting on to stretch the knees. The gunwale caps have been nailed.

MM #**88** L: 37" W: 7" D: 5"

TOP: Abenaki-Type Birchbark Canoe

Based on a canoe built by an Algonquin builder, Matt Bernard, at Golden Lake, Ontario, in 1905, and now at the Canadian Canoe Museum in Peterborough, Ontario. When the Canoe Museum acquired it, the canoe had been used as a poacher's canoe in Algonquin Park, Ontario. Adney built this model in 1927.

MM #**115** L: 29" W: 5⅞" D: 4"

BOTTOM: Abenaki-Type Ojibwa Birchbark Canoe

Based on a canoe built by an Ojibwa builder on the north shore of Lake Huron, east of Chapleau, Ontario. Adney built this model in 1930. The original canoe was built for the tourist trade. Nails are used at bow and stern, on the gunwales and caps and to secure the block decks. The webbed bow seat is a concession to sportsmen.

MM #**112** L: 33" W: 7" D: 4"

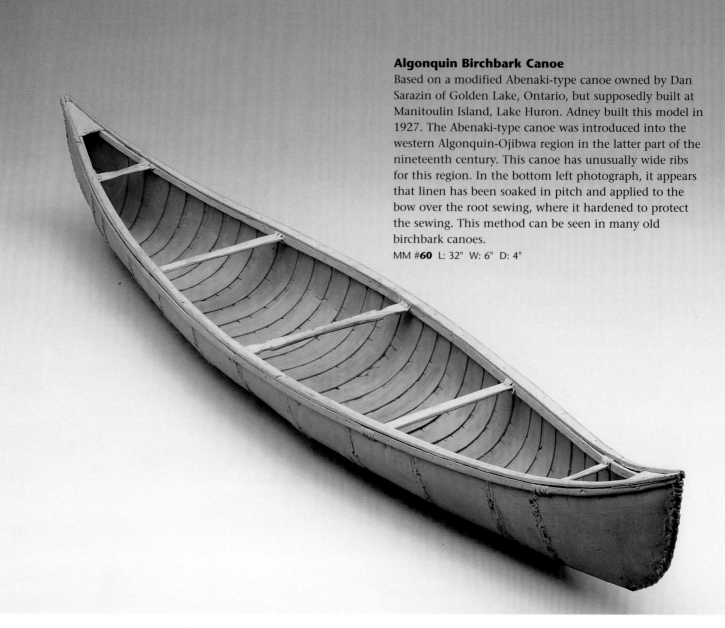

Algonquin Birchbark Canoe

Based on a modified Abenaki-type canoe owned by Dan Sarazin of Golden Lake, Ontario, but supposedly built at Manitoulin Island, Lake Huron. Adney built this model in 1927. The Abenaki-type canoe was introduced into the western Algonquin-Ojibwa region in the latter part of the nineteenth century. This canoe has unusually wide ribs for this region. In the bottom left photograph, it appears that linen has been soaked in pitch and applied to the bow over the root sewing, where it hardened to protect the sewing. This method can be seen in many old birchbark canoes.

MM #**60** L: 32" W: 6" D: 4"

Ottawa River Algonquin Birchbark Canoe
Based on a canoe built for William Huloff Jr. at the Golden Lake Reserve, Ontario, by Tom Sarazin in 1920. Adney built this model in 1927. The decoration is based on typical Algonquin images provided by Amab Sarazin in 1927. Tom Sarazin was one of the foremost canoe builders of his time and part of a great canoe-building dynasty. The Algonquin canoe builders of Maniwaki and Golden Lake remained expert builders long after the birchbark canoe-building tradition had died in most other Native communities.
MM #**83** L: 32" W: 7" D: 4⅞"

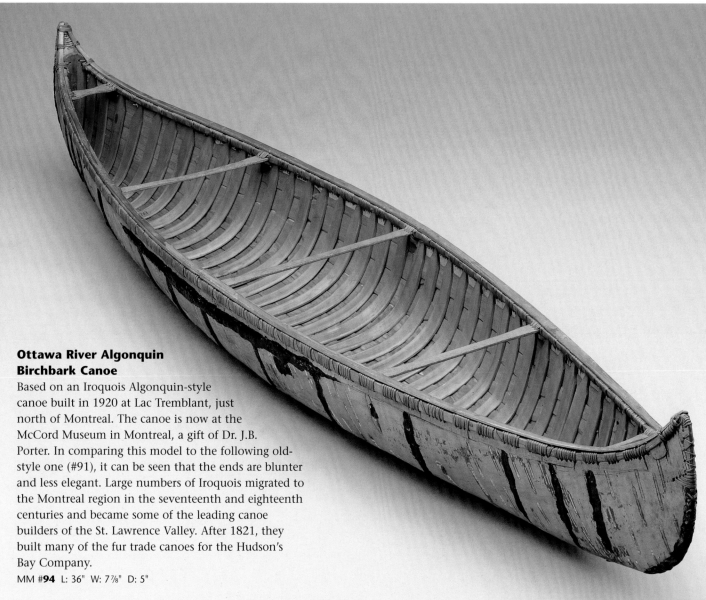

Ottawa River Algonquin Birchbark Canoe

Based on an Iroquois Algonquin-style canoe built in 1920 at Lac Tremblant, just north of Montreal. The canoe is now at the McCord Museum in Montreal, a gift of Dr. J.B. Porter. In comparing this model to the following old-style one (#91), it can be seen that the ends are blunter and less elegant. Large numbers of Iroquois migrated to the Montreal region in the seventeenth and eighteenth centuries and became some of the leading canoe builders of the St. Lawrence Valley. After 1821, they built many of the fur trade canoes for the Hudson's Bay Company.

MM #**94** L: 36" W: 7⅞" D: 5"

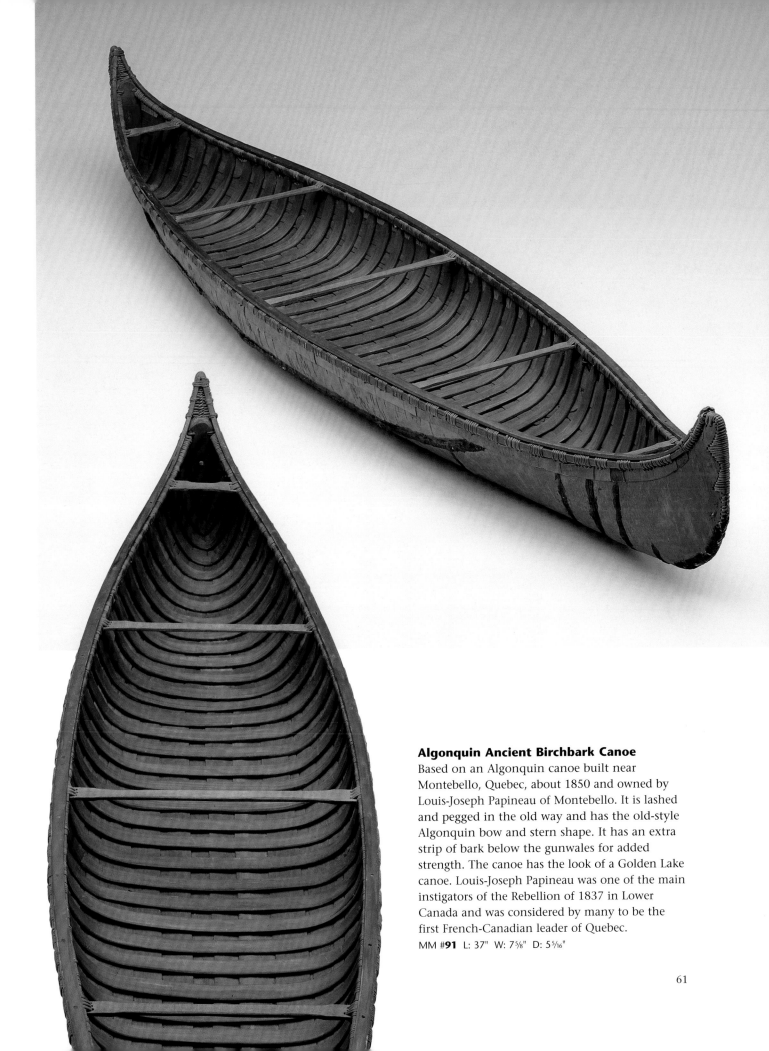

Algonquin Ancient Birchbark Canoe

Based on an Algonquin canoe built near
Montebello, Quebec, about 1850 and owned by
Louis-Joseph Papineau of Montebello. It is lashed
and pegged in the old way and has the old-style
Algonquin bow and stern shape. It has an extra
strip of bark below the gunwales for added
strength. The canoe has the look of a Golden Lake
canoe. Louis-Joseph Papineau was one of the main
instigators of the Rebellion of 1837 in Lower
Canada and was considered by many to be the
first French-Canadian leader of Quebec.

MM #**91** L: 37" W: 7⅝" D: 5⁵⁄₁₆"

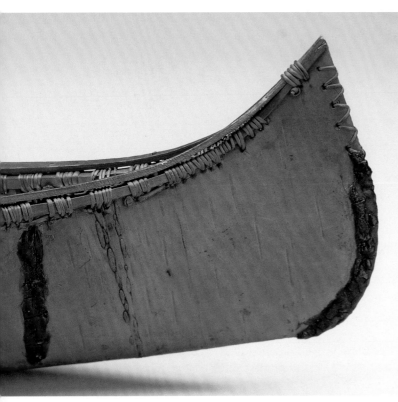

Têtes de Boule Two-Fathom Birchbark Hunter's Canoe

Based on two canoes from the upper St. Maurice River region, built in the mid-1920s by Testibaldi Pitiguay and Willie Chilton. The St. Maurice, a tributary of the St. Lawrence, is currently the site of one of North America's most renowned marathon canoe races, from La Tuque to Shawinigan. At the confluence of the St. Maurice and the St. Lawrence, the city of Trois-Rivières was the foremost center of fur trade canoe building for almost two centuries. The very fine ends of this canoe are similar to the Maliseet and Abenaki. The Têtes de Boule inhabited the region of the upper St. Maurice, Ottawa and Manouan Rivers and Grand Lake Victoria and Lake Barrière.

MM #**98** L: 31" W: 6⅛" D: 5"

Têtes de Boule One-Man Birchbark Hunter's Canoe

Based on a small hunting canoe built on the St. Maurice River in 1930 by a builder named Dube. Adney built this model in 1930. Except for the lower and blunter ends, it is a smaller version of #98 on the previous page. The Têtes de Boule, or White Fish people, were called "Round Heads" because they were the only Native group in the region who cut their hair short. Known as very good canoe builders, they had a long tradition of building canoes for the fur trade. Their canoes, although very similar to those of the St. Francis Abenaki, were generally narrower in the bottom and paddled very easily.

MM **#41** L: 20" W: 5" D: 4⅝"

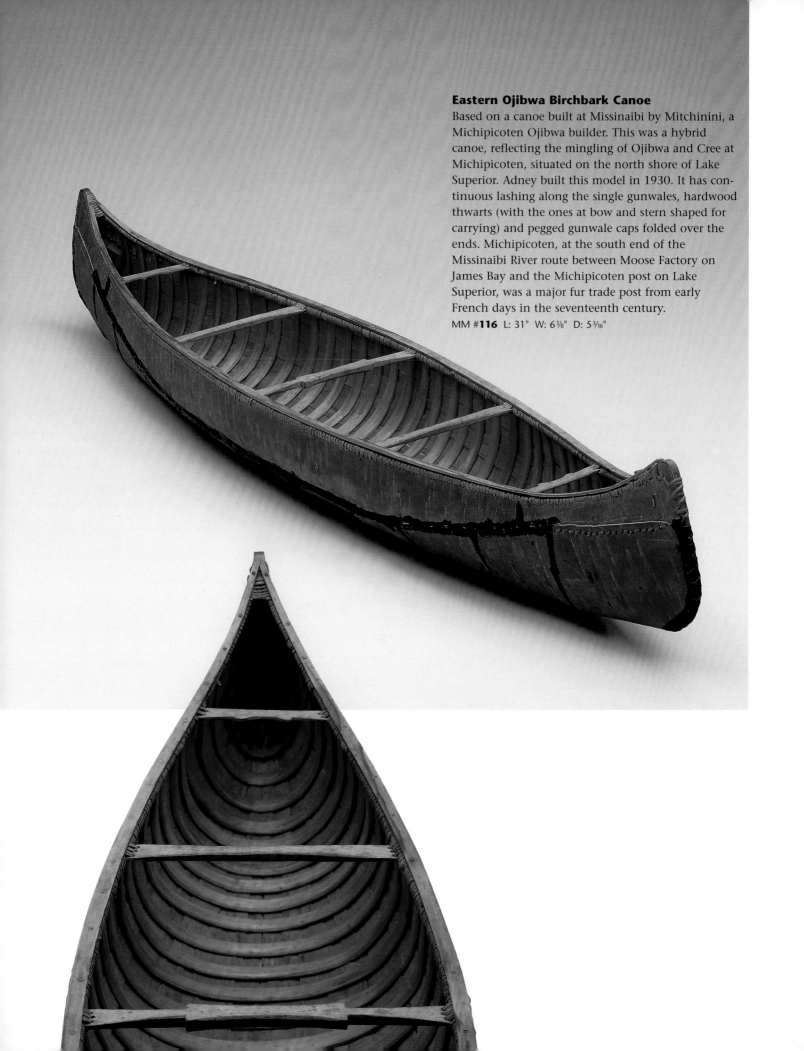

Eastern Ojibwa Birchbark Canoe
Based on a canoe built at Missinaibi by Mitchinini, a Michipicoten Ojibwa builder. This was a hybrid canoe, reflecting the mingling of Ojibwa and Cree at Michipicoten, situated on the north shore of Lake Superior. Adney built this model in 1930. It has continuous lashing along the single gunwales, hardwood thwarts (with the ones at bow and stern shaped for carrying) and pegged gunwale caps folded over the ends. Michipicoten, at the south end of the Missinaibi River route between Moose Factory on James Bay and the Michipicoten post on Lake Superior, was a major fur trade post from early French days in the seventeenth century.
MM #**116** L: 31" W: 6⅜" D: 5³⁄₁₆"

Eastern Ojibwa Birchbark Canoe

Based on an ancient Ojibwa model at the Peabody Museum, Harvard University, dated 1849. Adney built this model in 1927, faithfully creating all the elements of the Peabody model, but correcting its proportions. Native model builders generally did not worry about accurate dimensions. The gunwale caps are pegged and red ocher has been used on the thwarts and headboards, under the gunwales and in a line along the ribs — exactly as in the original model.

MM #**47** L: 33" W: 7⅜" D: 5"

Eastern Ojibwa Four-Fathom Birchbark Canoe

Based on a canoe built in about 1880 at Sault Ste. Marie and used principally for fishing whitefish. Adney built this model in 1938. The model, representing an unusually large Native canoe, is especially neat and the root lashing beautifully to scale, perhaps reflecting Adney's ever-advancing artistry, even in his seventies. This seven-thwart canoe was roughly the same size as a fur trade North Canoe. Similar canoes with lower ends and six bars, rather than seven, were used in Wisconsin for harvesting wild rice. The Ojibwa are a large group whose territory once extended from Lake Superior to Lake Winnipeg. South of Lake Superior they are known as the Chippewa and to the west as the Salteaux.

MM #**145** L: 57" W: 11" D: 9"

TOP: Eastern Ojibwa Birchbark Canoe
Based on a canoe at Lake Mississauga, Ontario, and on a Canadian Pacific Railway photograph titled "Mississauga Lake." Adney built this model in 1926. It has a typical Algonquin-type bow and stern. The notched center thwart is unusual for an Ojibwa canoe, but otherwise it is a very typical eastern Ojibwa type.
MM #**74** L: 34" W: 7⅛" D: 5⅝"

BOTTOM: Eastern Ojibwa Birchbark Canoe
Based on a full-scale canoe at the Peabody Museum, Harvard University, collected by Henry Gilman in 1873 at Lake Superior. Adney built this model in 1927. This is a typical eastern Ojibwa canoe, with pegged gunwale caps and group lashing. It represents the old form, similar to the Algonquin canoe, used by the Ojibwa north of Lake Superior.
MM #**136** L: 33" W: 7⅛" D: 6"

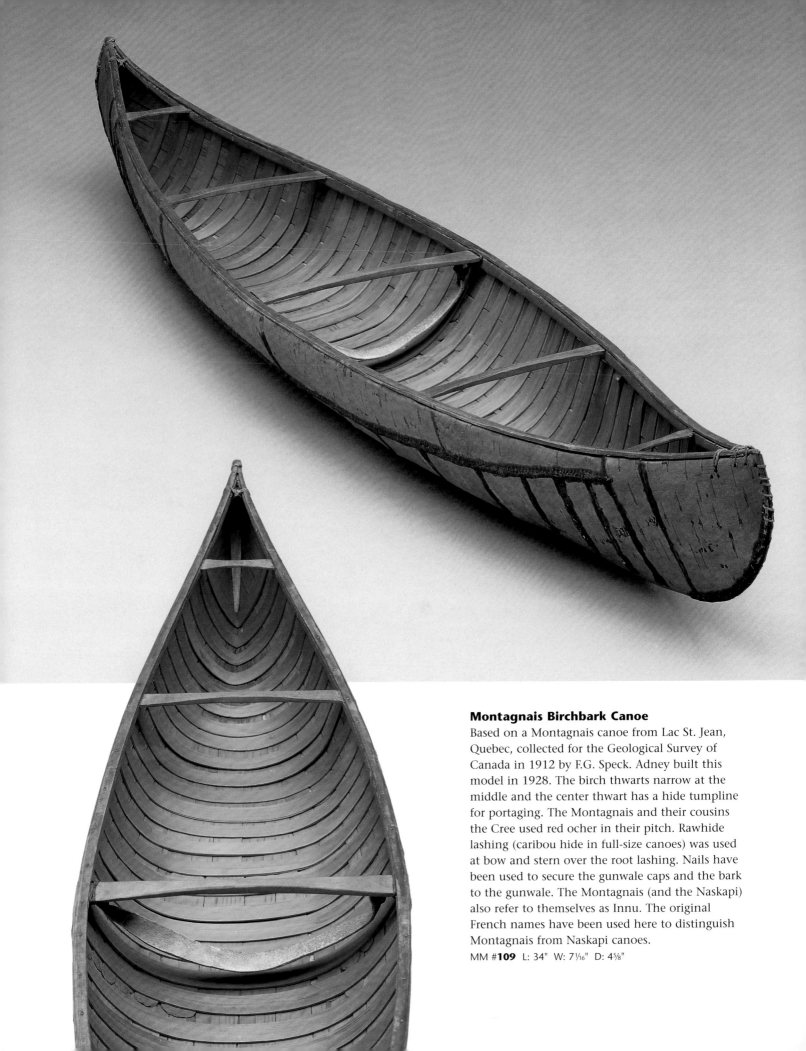

Montagnais Birchbark Canoe

Based on a Montagnais canoe from Lac St. Jean, Quebec, collected for the Geological Survey of Canada in 1912 by F.G. Speck. Adney built this model in 1928. The birch thwarts narrow at the middle and the center thwart has a hide tumpline for portaging. The Montagnais and their cousins the Cree used red ocher in their pitch. Rawhide lashing (caribou hide in full-size canoes) was used at bow and stern over the root lashing. Nails have been used to secure the gunwale caps and the bark to the gunwale. The Montagnais (and the Naskapi) also refer to themselves as Innu. The original French names have been used here to distinguish Montagnais from Naskapi canoes.

MM #**109** L: 34" W: 7¹⁄₁₆" D: 4⅝"

Montagnais Birchbark Canoe

Based on a Montagnais model at the Peabody Museum, Harvard University, dated 1849, and on the full-scale Montagnais canoe that #109 is based on. The painted exterior and thwarts exactly copy the Peabody model. Adney built this model before 1928. It is identical to the Peabody model in every detail except dimensions. Hide sewing has been used on bow and stern. The decorative dots seem to have no special significance. The Montagnais reside on the north shore of the St. Lawrence River and along its turbulent tributaries. They are still building traditional canoes with canvas covering at the St. Lawrence community of Romaine.

MM #**111**   L: 35"   W: 7⅛"   D: 5"

TOP: **Naskapi Crooked Canoe**

Based on Naskapi canoes from Great Whale River and Fort George (a Hudson's Bay Company post), Quebec, 1912. Also based on Canadian Pacific Railway photographs from 1912. Adney built this model before 1928. This is an example of a moderate crooked canoe, so named because of the curvature of the bottom. These canoes were very good on the shallow rocky rivers of northern Quebec, either shooting down through rapids or being poled upstream.

MM #**99** L: 36" W: 8" D: 6½"

BOTTOM: **Naskapi Canvas Crooked Canoe**

Based on a Geological Survey of Canada photograph by F.W. Waugh, 1921, at Natashquan River, Quebec. This is a canvas version of model #99 but with less rocker. This canoe would be considered a borderline crooked canoe. The gunwale caps and canvas have been nailed to the gunwale and the thwarts have been mortised into the gunwales. The ends of the canoe have been lashed with sinew, probably caribou.

MM #**110** L: 41" W: 7" D: 7"

Naskapi Birchbark Crooked Canoe

Based on a Geological Survey of Canada photograph by
A.P. Low in 1912 taken at the Hudson's Bay Company
post at Fort George, Quebec. This is a very good example
of the true crooked canoe. It could carry a heavy load and
still maneuver beautifully either up or down river. Some
crooked canoes were even more extreme than this one.
The many pieces of bark reflect the small trees of the
northern location. This is one of Adney's most refined
models. The split-root lashing on the gunwales is wonder-
fully to scale, as is the sinew sewing of the bark. The
Naskapi, a branch of the Eastern Cree, inhabit northern
Quebec and Labrador.

MM #**51** L: 39" W: 8" D: 9"

Eastern Cree Canvas Canoe

Based on a Geological Survey of Canada photograph, 1906–7, from the Albany River, Ontario. Adney built this model in 1924. It is puzzling that the canvas is sewn with root to the gunwales. Nails would have less tendency to rip out. It is also puzzling that two pieces of canvas have been used, painstakingly stitched together with what is probably sinew, which would have been used in the original. Another intriguing aspect of this model is that Adney called this a Winisk River canoe, from the west side of Hudson Bay, but it is clearly an Eastern Cree type. When Adney visited Rupert House in 1908, there was not a single birchbark canoe left; they were all canvas.

MM #**62** L: 35" W: 7" D: 4"

Cree Spruce Bark Canoe

Based on a canoe model from Fort Chimo, Quebec, built by a Cree builder and collected by Edward Peck of Montreal in 1910. Adney built this model in 1931. The sheathing is overlapping in the Cree style. The gunwale caps are secured with twine. Red ocher has been used to accent the canoe. Since birch trees were small and scarce that far north, the Cree often used spruce bark instead. It produced a passable canoe, but one that looked somewhat crude beside a good birchbark canoe. They could have looked even worse, but they were built with a number of strips of bark from gunwale to gunwale, thus allowing for more sophisticated shaping and strong attachment at the gunwales.

MM #**71**   L: 38" W: 7⅞" D: 5"

Winisk River Cree Spruce Bark Canoe

Based on a large Cree model from Mimigwes Lake, Ontario. It is assumed that Adney intentionally made these models look crude. Spruce bark cannot be finely shaped, but the root lashing is also quite crude. This canoe had an inner stempiece with continuous root lashing from the gunwales through the stems. The Cree of the Winisk region, known as the West Main Cree, were part of the Swampy Cree, one of the three major Cree groups who inhabited the area from northern Quebec to northeastern Manitoba.

MM #**54** L: 36" W: 7" D: 5⅜"

Eastern Cree Spruce Bark Canoe

Based on Winisk River, Ontario, and Fort Chimo, Quebec, canoes and on a model collected at Fort Chimo in 1910 by Hugh Peck of Montreal and now in the McCord Museum, Montreal. Adney built this model before 1928. It has overlapping sheathing and an outer stem assembly. The gunwale cap and stem are secured with hide. This canoe has a gunwale cap; the previous one does not. This detail was purely at the whim of the builder. It must be assumed that the extreme crudeness of the gunwale lashing was intentional. The oblong patches of vermillion paint on the gunwale caps and at the end of the thwarts were very typical. The spruce paddles were decorated in the same way.

MM #**137** L: 34" W: 7" D: 4⅞"

Western Ojibwa Birchbark Canoe
Based on an Ojibwa canoe from Bois Fort Reserve, Minnesota, now at the Canadian Museum of Civilization. Adney built this model in 1928. The canoe is unusual in having both gunwale caps and an outwale to protect the continuous lashing. The caps are nailed and red ocher has been used instead of pitch; the gores are not real.
MM #**70** L: 34" W: 7⅛" D: 5"

76

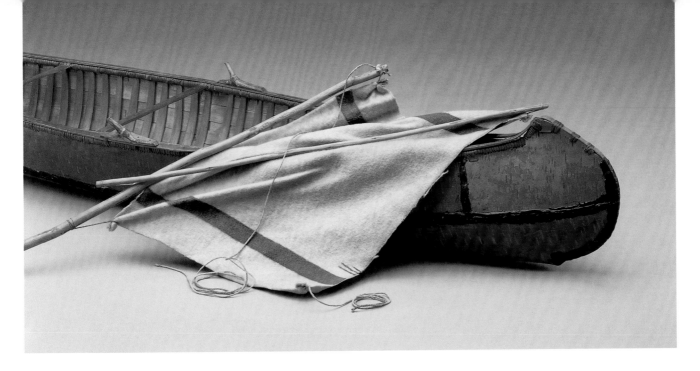

Lake Nipigon Western Ojibwa Birchbark Canoe
Based on a Lake Nipigon Ojibwa canoe of the mid-1890s for transporting sportsmen. The canoe has a mast, spar and a square sail made from a two-and-a-half-point Hudson's Bay Company trade blanket. The value of the trade blanket was woven into it in the form of fine lines (next to the lower wide black bar). The canoe also has oarlocks fashioned from notched birch branches.

MM #**123** L: 43" W: 8⅝" D: 6"

TOP: Western Ojibwa Birchbark Canoe

Based on canoes from the Leech Lake and Red Lake, Minnesota, region and on one from the Bois Fort Reserve, now in the Canadian Museum of Civilization. Adney built this model in 1929. This canoe is a hybrid type, combining the shape of the western Ojibwa canoe with the double gunwale, group lashing and gunwale cap of the eastern Ojibwa canoe.

MM #**58** L: 36" W: 6⅞" D: 5⅛"

MIDDLE: Western Ojibwa Rice-Harvesting Birchbark Canoe

Based on an Ojibwa canoe from Long Lake, Ontario, now in the Canadian Museum of Civilization. Adney built this model in 1926. Wild rice–harvesting canoes did not have a middle portaging thwart. Rice was both a staple food and a major trade item.

MM #**73** L: 37" W: 7⅛" D: 6"

BOTTOM: Western Cree Rice-Harvesting Birchbark Canoe

Based on a 1 to 4 Cree model from Mimigwes Lake, Winisk River, Ontario. Adney gave this model to the Château de Ramezay Museum in Montreal. Adney built this model in 1927. Usually two women gathered the wild rice. One bent the rice over the gunwale and the other knocked the heads off into the canoe.

MM #**114** L: 35" W: 6⅞" D: 5⅝"

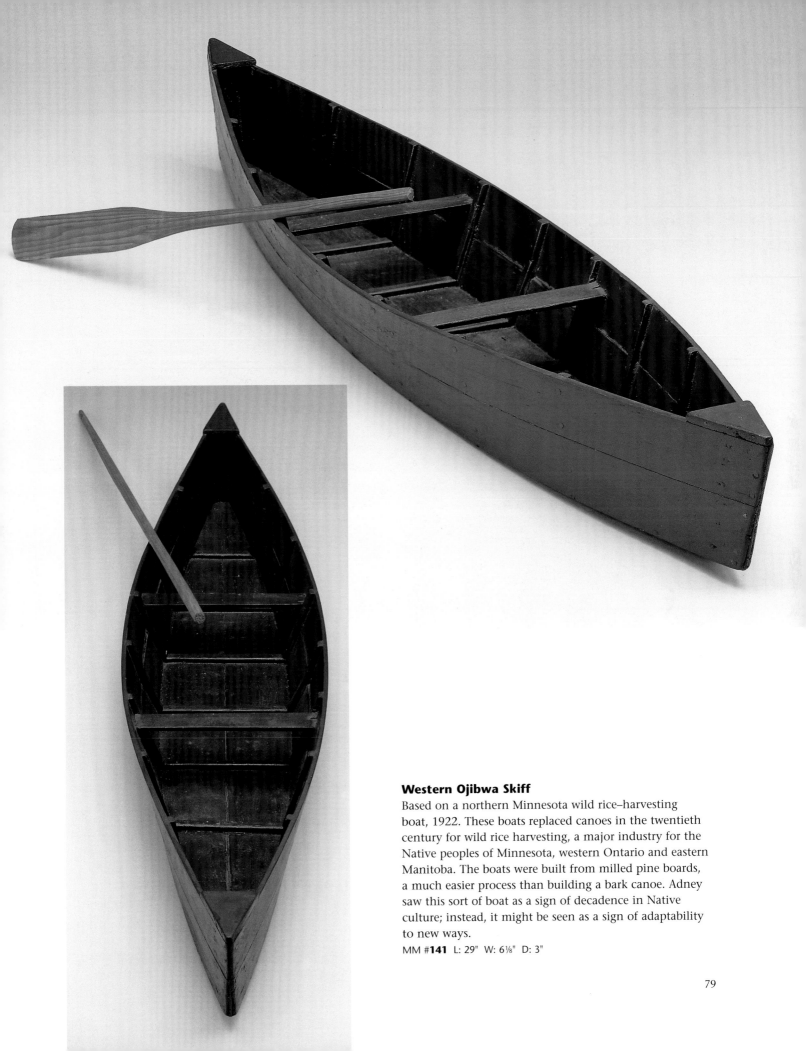

Western Ojibwa Skiff

Based on a northern Minnesota wild rice–harvesting boat, 1922. These boats replaced canoes in the twentieth century for wild rice harvesting, a major industry for the Native peoples of Minnesota, western Ontario and eastern Manitoba. The boats were built from milled pine boards, a much easier process than building a bark canoe. Adney saw this sort of boat as a sign of decadence in Native culture; instead, it might be seen as a sign of adaptability to new ways.

MM #**141** L: 29" W: 6⅛" D: 3"

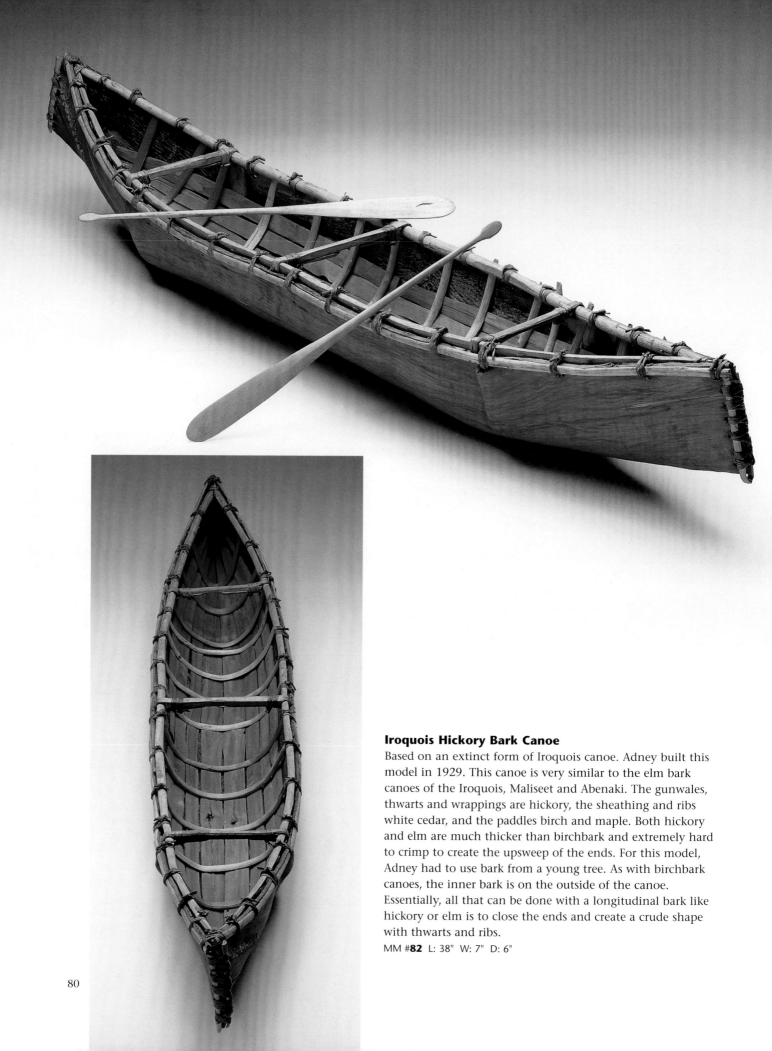

Iroquois Hickory Bark Canoe

Based on an extinct form of Iroquois canoe. Adney built this model in 1929. This canoe is very similar to the elm bark canoes of the Iroquois, Maliseet and Abenaki. The gunwales, thwarts and wrappings are hickory, the sheathing and ribs white cedar, and the paddles birch and maple. Both hickory and elm are much thicker than birchbark and extremely hard to crimp to create the upsweep of the ends. For this model, Adney had to use bark from a young tree. As with birchbark canoes, the inner bark is on the outside of the canoe. Essentially, all that can be done with a longitudinal bark like hickory or elm is to close the ends and create a crude shape with thwarts and ribs.

MM #**82** L: 38" W: 7" D: 6"

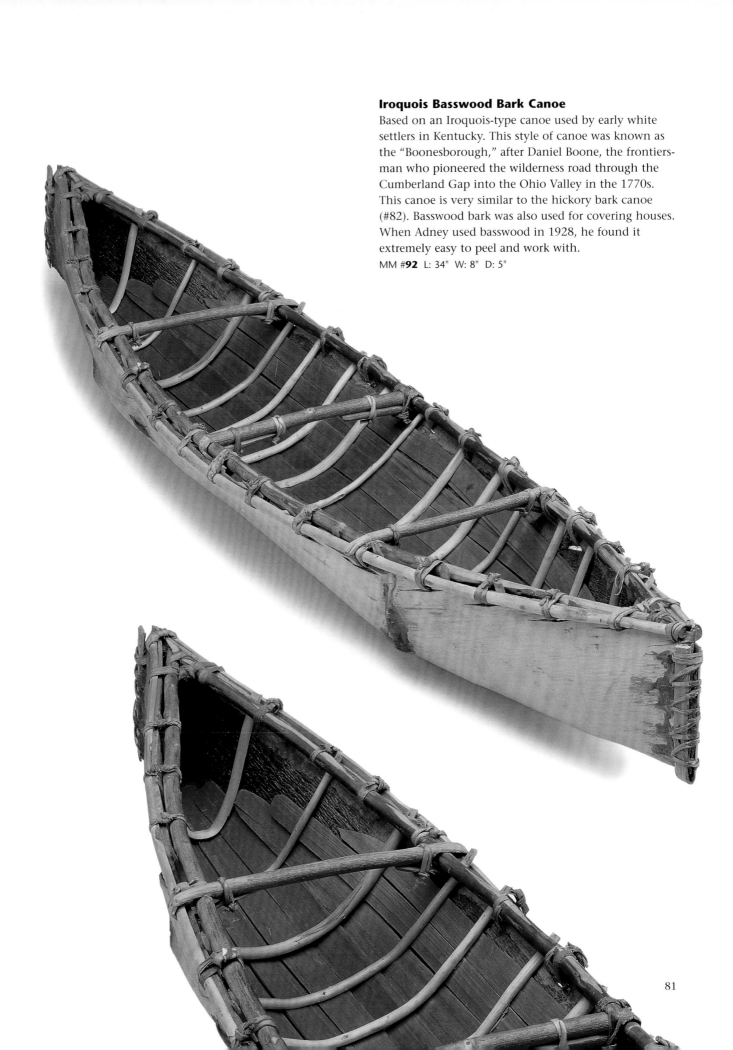

Iroquois Basswood Bark Canoe
Based on an Iroquois-type canoe used by early white settlers in Kentucky. This style of canoe was known as the "Boonesborough," after Daniel Boone, the frontiersman who pioneered the wilderness road through the Cumberland Gap into the Ohio Valley in the 1770s. This canoe is very similar to the hickory bark canoe (#82). Basswood bark was also used for covering houses. When Adney used basswood in 1928, he found it extremely easy to peel and work with.
MM #**92** L: 34" W: 8" D: 5"

Iroquois Elm Bark Canoe

Based on an Iroquois canoe at the Canadian Museum of Civilization. This canoe has a double gunwale of alder poles, sheathing of alder or maple saplings, a sapling stempiece and bark stitching. The Iroquois of upper New York State lived south of the region of the birch tree and had to make do with elm bark and dugout canoes. Elm bark canoes, like those of spruce, had to be built with speed because the bark dried out quickly and became hard to work with. In the early seventeenth century, the explorer Samuel de Champlain described Iroquois elm bark war canoes longer than 30 feet made from one piece of bark. The Iroquois were not known as canoeing people until they migrated north to birchbark country.

MM #**147** L: 34⅛" W: 7⅞" D: 5"

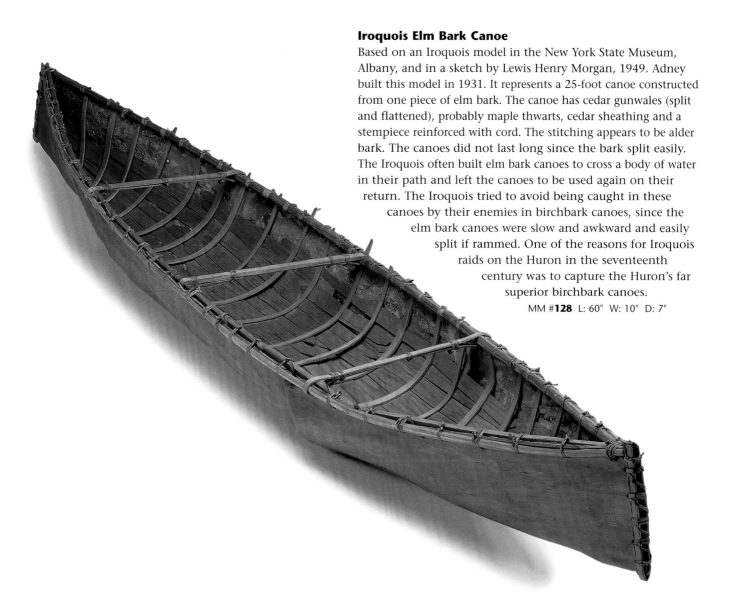

Iroquois Elm Bark Canoe

Based on an Iroquois model in the New York State Museum, Albany, and in a sketch by Lewis Henry Morgan, 1949. Adney built this model in 1931. It represents a 25-foot canoe constructed from one piece of elm bark. The canoe has cedar gunwales (split and flattened), probably maple thwarts, cedar sheathing and a stempiece reinforced with cord. The stitching appears to be alder bark. The canoes did not last long since the bark split easily. The Iroquois often built elm bark canoes to cross a body of water in their path and left the canoes to be used again on their return. The Iroquois tried to avoid being caught in these canoes by their enemies in birchbark canoes, since the elm bark canoes were slow and awkward and easily split if rammed. One of the reasons for Iroquois raids on the Huron in the seventeenth century was to capture the Huron's far superior birchbark canoes.

MM #**128** L: 60" W: 10" D: 7"

CANOES OF THE
Northwest

The Native peoples of the Northwest and Alaska had two basic types of bark canoe, one unique to the region and the other sharing similarities with eastern bark canoes. The first type, especially those of the Gwich'in, showed closer affinities to Inuit kayaks than to canoes of the East Coast and Eastern Woodlands. Adney did not know these canoes as well as he knew the canoes of the East Coast and Eastern Woodlands, but his papers show clearly that he read all the possible historical literature on the region, tried to find examples in American and Canadian museums, and corresponded with a number of people who might know something about the canoes of the Northwest. The fur trade arrived in the Northwest in 1778 in the form of the infamous Peter Pond, who was the first fur trader to be taken over the Methye Portage, the longest portage in Canada east of the Rocky Mountains, and into the Athabaska country of the Chipewyans. Fort Chipewyan, at the outlet of Lake Athabasca, soon became the focal point of the fur trade. It is likely that the canoes of the fur trade influenced Northwestern canoe builders after the beginning of the nineteenth century, though it is also likely that the Western Cree who had traded into the Northwest long before the fur trade arrived had already influenced the latter type of Northwestern canoe.

Chipewyan Birchbark Canoe

Based on Chipewyan hunting canoes, which were usually from 12 to 18 feet in length. Decoration details are from a drawing by Samuel Hearne. The interior structure of these Northwest canoes is closer to that of the Inuit kayak than the Eastern Woodland canoe. The stringers and keelson are held in place by pressure from the ribs. The canoe has double gunwales with group lashing similar to the canoes of the St. Lawrence. The floating bow deck is held with lashing only at the ends. Otherwise, it is bent over the gunwale using a hot ember to make it curl tightly in the opposite direction to its growth. The subtle longitudinal groove on both decks just inside the gunwale is made with the thumbnail. The curled bark attached to the bow deck, unique to the canoes of the Northwest, acts as a splash guard. A reinforcement "leaf" is used at the ends under the rawhide lashing. This canoe is very similar to those of the Dogrib.

MM #**56** L: 31¾" W: 5⅝" D: 3¼"

Chipewyan Birchbark Canoe

Based on a canoe from the Mackenzie River region now at the Canadian Museum of Civilization, Ottawa. Adney built this model before 1928. It is very similar to the previous one. It, too, could be a Dogrib canoe. The thwarts are mortised through both gunwales and pegged between them. The stringers and keelson are floating, held in only by the pressure of the ribs. The decks, too, are floating, held on by the reverse curve of the bark. The stem is typical of the Northwest, a solid piece of wood cut from the knee of a tree (where the grain curves at the join of a branch and trunk), and drilled through to accept the lashing. A canoe of this size in the Northwest would have used between 20 and 25 pieces of bark. These canoes were extremely light and delicate and, as with Inuit kayaks, easily punctured. This kayak form was well suited for hunting caribou or moose as they crossed rivers and lakes. The canoe was extremely responsive and could be steered with one hand as the other was busy with spear or knife. This is an unfinished model; it has not yet been gummed.

MM #**50** L: 29¼" W: 4⅛" D: 3⅛"

Chipewyan Birchbark Canoe

Based on a photo by F. Harper, 1914, in the photo collection of the Canadian Museum of Civilization. This is a canoe of the Taltson River–Great Slave Lake region. Adney built this model before 1928. This is a general-purpose family or cargo canoe. The influence of eastern canoes is evident in this type of Northwestern canoe: continuous lashing on the gunwales, pegged gunwale caps, eastern thwart lashing, headboards and sheathing and an upsweep to the lashed ends that is very unlike the Northwestern hunting canoes. The gunwale caps are pegged and lashed at the ends with rawhide.

MM #**79** L: 36" W: 6⅞" D: 4½"

Chipewyan Birchbark Canoe

Based on a Chipewyan canoe from North River, near Fort Churchill on Hudson Bay, collected by Christian Laden in 1914 and now at the Canadian Museum of Civilization. Partially visible on the pieces of red metal at the ends are the words "Hudson's Bay Company, Incorporated, May 1670." This canoe is similar to #79 (p. 87), but has nailed gunwales and no gunwale caps. The square sail is fashioned from a two-and-a-half-point Hudson's Bay Company trade blanket. This canoe was obviously built for carrying loads. Chipewyan canoes of this type were strongly influenced by the Cree, who came into the area before the fur trade in the late eighteenth century. The Cree probably introduced sails, which were used widely by Native peoples after European contact.

MM #**57** L: 39½" W: 7⅞" D: 5"

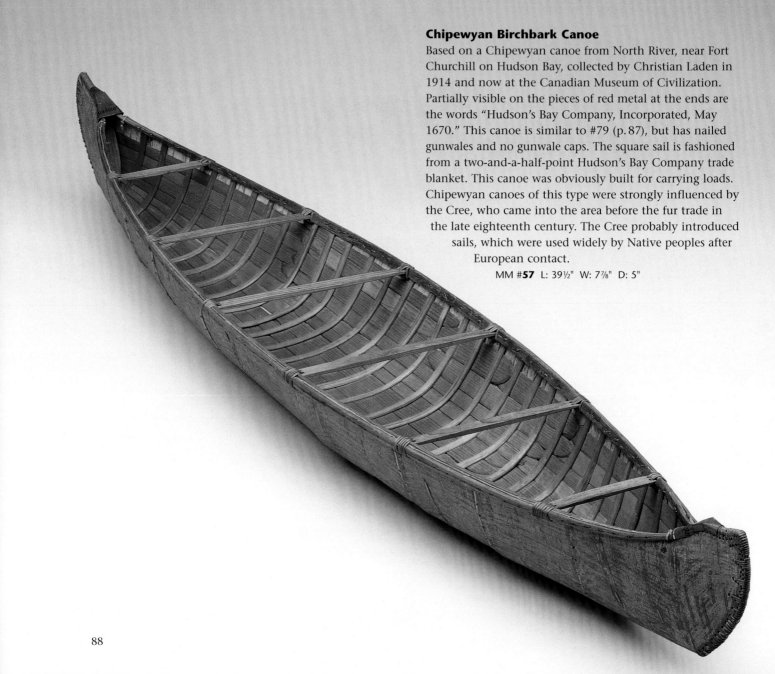

Northern Cree Birchbark Canoe

Based on a model at the Peabody Museum, Harvard University, marked "Northwestern Cree." Cree coming into the upper Mackenzie River and Churchill River regions adopted this local form of Athapascan canoe. It is similar to Eastern Woodland canoes in the sheathing and headboards, but shows the western building techniques of mortising the thwarts through both gunwales and pegging them between the gunwales. The canoe also has a solid protruding piece of wood for the stems. Rawhide was used to secure the ends of the outwales. For hundreds of years, Cree in canoes like these had been the main trading partners of the Hudson's Bay Company, making an annual trip with their furs to Hudson Bay. It was not until the end of the eighteenth century that the HBC began to venture inland to establish posts among other peoples.

MM #**105** L: 39" W: 5⅜" D: 4½"

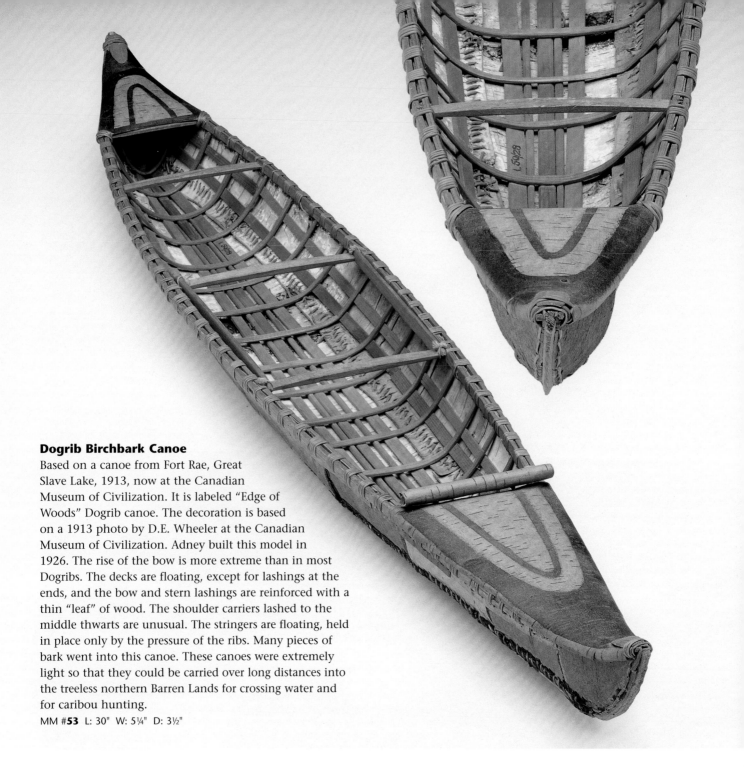

Dogrib Birchbark Canoe

Based on a canoe from Fort Rae, Great
Slave Lake, 1913, now at the Canadian
Museum of Civilization. It is labeled "Edge of
Woods" Dogrib canoe. The decoration is based
on a 1913 photo by D.E. Wheeler at the Canadian
Museum of Civilization. Adney built this model in
1926. The rise of the bow is more extreme than in most
Dogribs. The decks are floating, except for lashings at the
ends, and the bow and stern lashings are reinforced with a
thin "leaf" of wood. The shoulder carriers lashed to the
middle thwarts are unusual. The stringers are floating, held
in place only by the pressure of the ribs. Many pieces of
bark went into this canoe. These canoes were extremely
light so that they could be carried over long distances into
the treeless northern Barren Lands for crossing water and
for caribou hunting.

MM #**53** L: 30" W: 5¼" D: 3½"

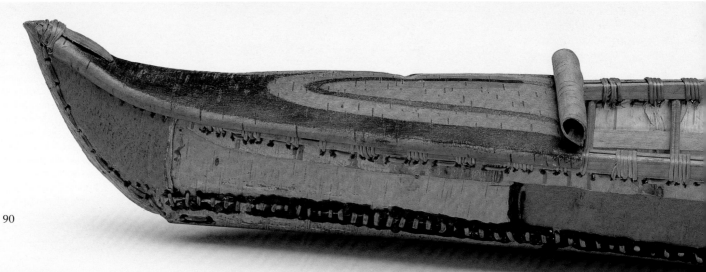

Dogrib Birchbark Canoe

Based on two Geological Survey of Canada photos, 1913, by J.A. Mason from the Great Slave Lake region and on a Dogrib canoe at the Canadian Museum of Civilization. Adney built this model before 1928. It represents an all-purpose family canoe. Adney has left the model ungummed. The gunwales, thwarts, head-boards, sheathing and pegged gunwale caps are similar to eastern canoes. The sheathing of black spruce was much harder to split than cedar. The "dimple" at the top of the plank stems is common to the whole Northwestern region. As in most of these canoes, there is a reinforcing strip of bark below the gunwales. This is a large, very beamy canoe of the kind seen in old photographs loaded down with the whole family, dogs and camp gear.

MM #**44** L: 50" W: 9½" D: 5¾"

Slavey Birchbark Canoe

Based on Geological Survey of Canada photos, 1916, by Charles Camsell at Hay River, Northwest Territories, and on a Slavey model collected by the Church Missionary Society. This canoe is similar to those built at Great Bear Lake. Adney built this model in 1926. This general-purpose canoe combines eastern and western features. The gunwales, thwarts, headboards and sheathing are very similar to eastern canoes. The solid protruding stempiece identifies it as a Northwestern canoe. The stempieces are unusually steep, and the sides have an extreme flare. This is a large canoe (16½ feet long). The fact that there is no bilge seam in the bark indicates that the original canoe was made from trade bark brought into the country. Good bark from the south was much sought after in northern regions where trees were small and bark thin.

MM #**131** L: 39¼" W: 8⁵⁄₁₆" D: 5¾"

Slavey Birchbark Canoe

Based on canoes of the upper Mackenzie River region at the end of the nineteenth century. Adney built this model in 1932. As with the previous canoe (#131), it is a mixture of eastern and western influences. The double gunwales, pegged gunwale caps and lashed thwarts are similar to eastern canoes. The protruding stempieces (the solid, wide and thin plates to which the bark is lashed) are definitely Northwestern. The canoe has an unusually large reinforcing panel of winter bark, with a zigzag pattern etched in the bark. The gunwale caps have been lashed with rawhide where they meet the stempieces. The canoe is even more flared than the previous one.

MM #**66** L: 45⅜" W: 9¼" D: 5⅜"

Upper Yukon Gwich'in Birchbark Hunting Canoe

Based on Adney's detailed drawings of this type of canoe when he was in the Klondike in 1897–98. (His drawing of this canoe is reproduced on page 23). The Gwich'in canoes are unique among Northwestern canoes in having a rigid frame, with the stringers held in place by crosspieces. Adney has used blocks between the stringers, but in a real canoe, the crosspiece would have been one piece of wood. The double gunwales of spruce are held together by continuous lashing. Each pair of gunwales is a single piece which has been split along its entire length, except at the ends, where the two gunwales are lashed together with rawhide. This would take great craftsmanship. The bow deck is completely floating, held only by the strong reverse curl of the bark. The elegant raking stems are unique to the Gwich'in.

These canoes were extremely light and fast. An 1869 sketch by Frederick Whymper shows a Gwich'in hunter leaning out of his canoe and killing a moose with a knife, while steering with his other hand.

MM #**63** L: 39⅜" W: 5½" D: 4¾"

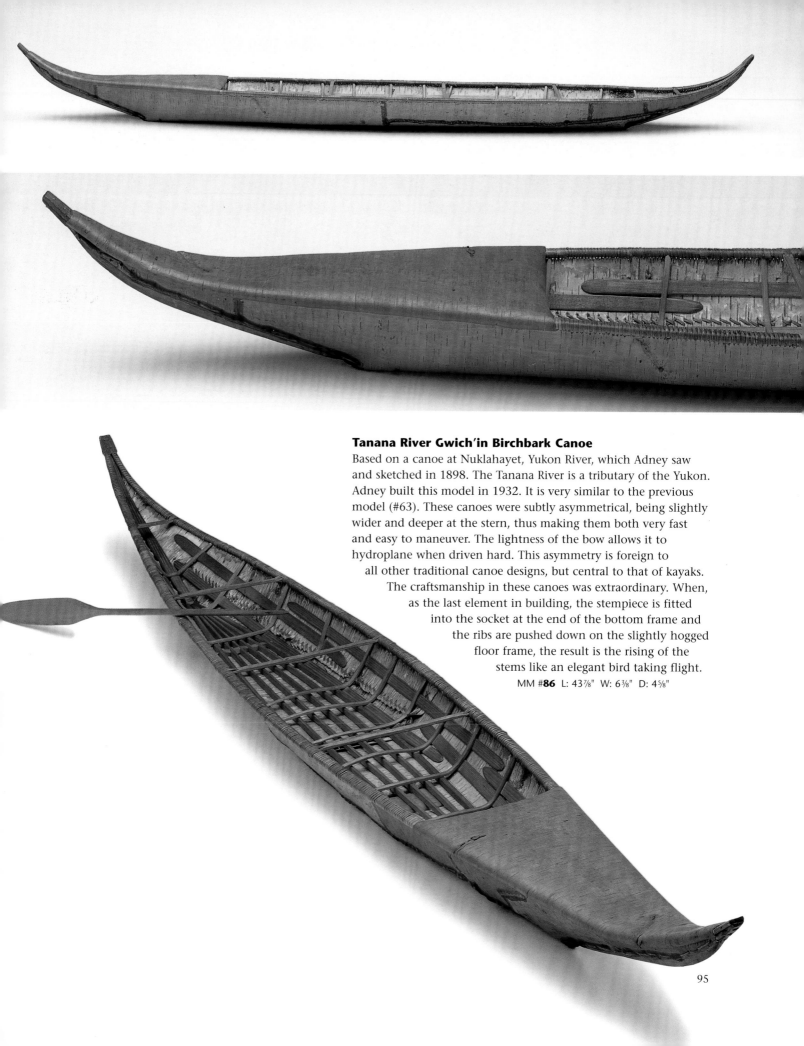

Tanana River Gwich'in Birchbark Canoe

Based on a canoe at Nuklahayet, Yukon River, which Adney saw and sketched in 1898. The Tanana River is a tributary of the Yukon. Adney built this model in 1932. It is very similar to the previous model (#63). These canoes were subtly asymmetrical, being slightly wider and deeper at the stern, thus making them both very fast and easy to maneuver. The lightness of the bow allows it to hydroplane when driven hard. This asymmetry is foreign to all other traditional canoe designs, but central to that of kayaks.

The craftsmanship in these canoes was extraordinary. When, as the last element in building, the stempiece is fitted into the socket at the end of the bottom frame and the ribs are pushed down on the slightly hogged floor frame, the result is the rising of the stems like an elegant bird taking flight.

MM #**86** L: 43⅞" W: 6⅜" D: 4⅝"

Middle Yukon Gwich'in Canvas Canoe

Based on a canvas canoe from Fort
Yukon, Alaska, 1922. It is hard to believe
that the same people built this canoe and
the previous two. This was a utilitarian
retrieval canoe, used for collecting geese or
muskrats or for fishing. There is no artistry
in this canoe but it is very solidly made by a
good builder. The gunwales, stringers and
ribs appear to be made from sawn lumber
and the nailed ribs indicate that the craft
was built after Europeans introduced the use
of nails. The thwarts are attached with
rawhide. Red ocher has been used extensively
on the canoe.

MM #**93** L: 24" W: 5⅜" D: 3"

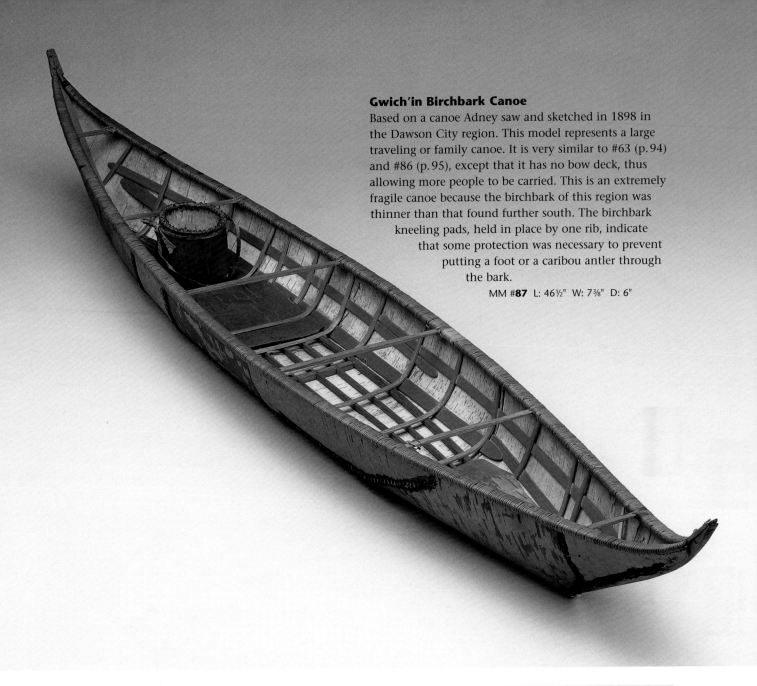

Gwich'in Birchbark Canoe

Based on a canoe Adney saw and sketched in 1898 in the Dawson City region. This model represents a large traveling or family canoe. It is very similar to #63 (p. 94) and #86 (p. 95), except that it has no bow deck, thus allowing more people to be carried. This is an extremely fragile canoe because the birchbark of this region was thinner than that found further south. The birchbark kneeling pads, held in place by one rib, indicate that some protection was necessary to prevent putting a foot or a caribou antler through the bark.

MM #**87** L: 46½" W: 7⅜" D: 6"

Athapascan Birchbark Canoe

Based on an 1849 model of a Fraser River Athapascan canoe at the Peabody Museum, Harvard University, purchased in 1905 through the Walcott Fund. People stopped making this type of canoe long ago. Adney built this model in 1927. A careful comparison with the Peabody model shows that Adney copied this model in every detail, as was his practice when copying either models or full-scale canoes. The canoe has cedar ribs, held in place by rawhide lashed to a stringer behind the ribs in a fashion similar to Inuit kayaks. Unique to this model is the material interwoven in the gunwale wrapping. Adney mentioned in his notes that the Athapascans sometimes used dyed grass for this purpose. The groove on the thwarts could be for identification. Grooves are very common in the Arctic for identifying implements. Ocher has been used on the solid stempieces and the thwarts and in a line above the rawhide lashing.

MM #**49** L: 43" W: 8½" D: 6½"

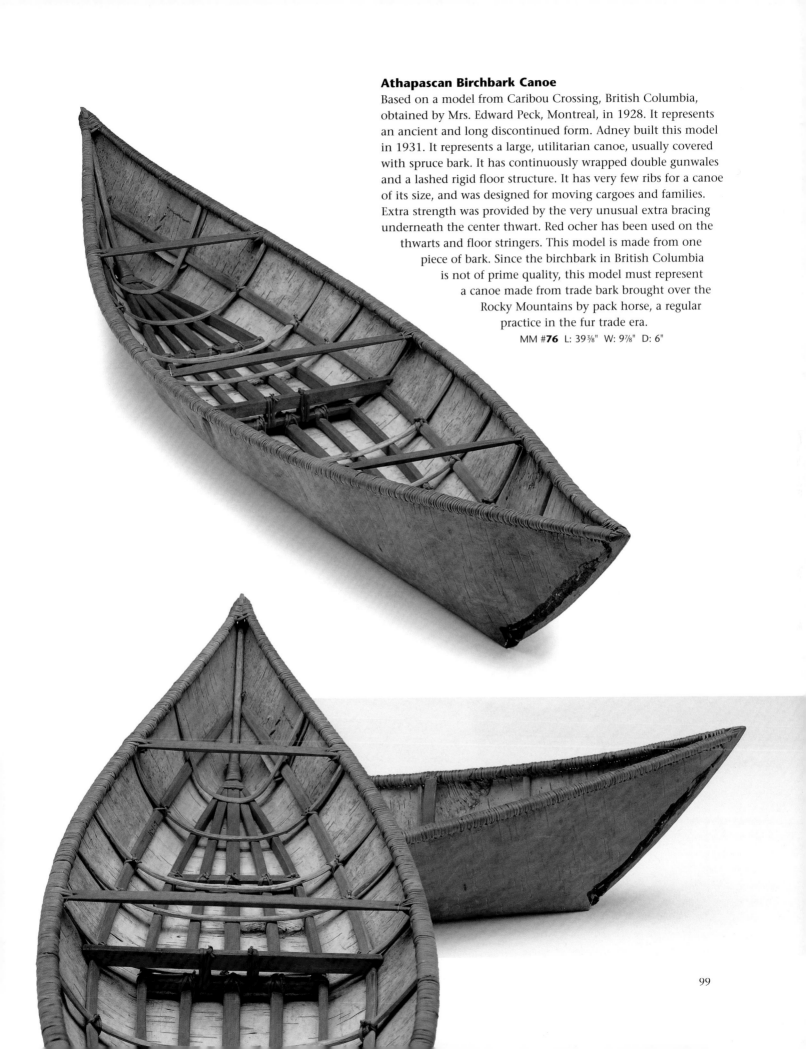

Athapascan Birchbark Canoe

Based on a model from Caribou Crossing, British Columbia, obtained by Mrs. Edward Peck, Montreal, in 1928. It represents an ancient and long discontinued form. Adney built this model in 1931. It represents a large, utilitarian canoe, usually covered with spruce bark. It has continuously wrapped double gunwales and a lashed rigid floor structure. It has very few ribs for a canoe of its size, and was designed for moving cargoes and families. Extra strength was provided by the very unusual extra bracing underneath the center thwart. Red ocher has been used on the thwarts and floor stringers. This model is made from one piece of bark. Since the birchbark in British Columbia is not of prime quality, this model must represent a canoe made from trade bark brought over the Rocky Mountains by pack horse, a regular practice in the fur trade era.

MM #**76** L: 39⅜" W: 9⅞" D: 6"

Athapascan Spruce Bark Canoe

Based on a birchbark model from Lake Atlin, British Columbia, obtained at Caribou Crossing, B.C., in 1928 and now at the McCord Museum, Montreal. This type of canoe, long extinct, was probably used by the Carrier, Sikani, Beaver and Tehani of the Liard River, Yukon Territory. Adney built this model in 1931. This was a very temporary craft, with minimum gunwale lashing to avoid splitting the bark. The double gunwales of carved poles are in a vertical plane with the bark between, bent slightly to the outside for extra support. The bilge stringers and keelson have been lashed to an extra brace. The stems are merely boards, lashed to the bilge stringers and keelson. Altogether, not an elegant canoe, but one of simple ingenuity and sturdiness, which could be built from spruce bark without having to shape it.

MM #**77** L: 36¾" W: 9¼" D: 6"

Athapascan Birchbark Canoe

Based on a Native model at the McCord Museum, Montreal, obtained in 1928 at Carcross, Yukon Territory. This was a type of canoe probably used in the interior of British Columbia and the lower Yukon Territory. Adney built this model in 1929. It is similar to the previous model (#77), except for the gunwale wrapping. The keelson and bilge stringers are made from extremely bulky sawn timbers. It, too, has an extra brace below the center thwart, which may be unique to Athapascan canoes. The longer rake of the bow is typical of Athapascan canoes.

MM #**78**   L: 34⅛"   W: 8⅛"   D: 5¹³⁄₁₆"

Carrier Birchbark Canoe

Based on a model of an extinct type from northern British Columbia, acquired by Hayter Reed of the Canadian Pacific Railway in 1890 from the Fraser River region. Adney built this model in 1932. It is a truly amazing canoe. It has double gunwales that have been fashioned from one piece of spruce that has been very carefully split in four longitudinal sections up to the single black end pieces. The stringers are held just by the pressure of the ribs. Two darker longitudinal lengths of spruce root on each side have been interwoven into the continuous gunwale wrapping. Red ocher has been applied at the ends of the thwarts, below the gunwales and on the stempieces, which were probably taken from the knee of a tree to get the curve of the grain. Thin strips of wood have been added to the deck and pegged down. The exquisite craftsmanship and decoration suggest that the original canoe must have belonged to someone very important.

MM #**107** L: 27½" W: 6¼" D: 6¼"

Malemut Birchbark Canoe

Based on a canoe that Adney saw in
1898 in an Inuit community on the lower
Yukon River. Adney referred to this craft as a
birchbark kayak. Certainly there are striking
similarities with Inuit kayaks, but this canoe also
has many characteristics of Dogrib and Gwich'in
canoes. The gunwales, lashing and floor frame are typical of Gwich'in canoes. The rawhide reinforcement of
the thwarts is unusual, as is the longitudinal strip of
spruce root under the lashing of the stern deck. Adney
also made a dog harness and towing line for this model.
Huskies were often used to pull a canoe upstream from
shore. This canoe might represent a trade canoe of the
Gwich'in people, though Adney claimed that the Inuit of
the Yukon used birchbark kayaks on rivers and sealskin
ones on the ocean. Gwich'in territory adjoined that of
the Inuit of the lower Yukon.

MM #**55** L: 34¼" W: 5½" D: 4"

CANOES OF
Asia and South America

Adney tried to include in his research and model-building a comprehensive comparison of all bark canoes in the world. A few of the canoes in this section are somewhat conjectural and he has not included the eucalyptus bark canoe of Australia. Otherwise, this section covers all the bark canoe types around the world of which he was aware. Adney tried very hard, both personally and through contacts, to get information from Russian sources on the bark canoes of eastern Russia. He was met with a wall of silence. Since the canoes of the Amur River region of eastern Russia and China were so similar to those of the Kootenay and Shuswap of British Columbia and the American Northwest, this silence was extremely frustrating.

Adney's contention that birchbark is the only bark capable of producing a sophisticated canoe becomes very clear in this section. The long-extinct birchbark canoes of the Amur peoples were the only ones outside North America that could be considered to be on a technological level with those of Canada and the northern United States. There are many canoes in this section that show great ingenuity in their construction, but all, except the Amur canoes, demonstrate Adney's contention that all forms of bark other than birchbark are very limited as construction material.

Shuswap Sturgeon-Nose Spruce Bark Canoe
Based on a model made by a Shuswap builder at Sicamous, Shuswap Lake, British Columbia, and given to Colonel E. Forrester of Victoria, British Columbia, in 1895. Adney built this model in 1927. The Shuswap people live in the region of the Fraser and Thompson rivers and used canoes similar to the canoes of their neighbors, the Carriers. This canoe was very similar to the Kootenay canoes, but did not have the birchbark strake at the gunwales. Instead, it had an ingenious way of avoiding the rib pressure that might rip the bark at the gunwales. It had a structure of floating ribs lashed to stringers, which in turn were held in place by very few ribs. The gunwales, thwarts and end closings were the same as in the Kootenay canoes. The seams were caulked with moss.
MM #**43** L: 35¼" W: 7¾" D: 5"

Kootenay Sturgeon-Nose Canvas Canoe

Based on a canoe built by the Kootenay people of lower B.C. and the northwestern United States in the 1940s. This canoe and the other three from British Columbia and Washington state are placed in this section because they are unlike any other canoes in North America. They are, however, strikingly similar to the bark canoes of the Amur River of Asia, which forms the eastern boundary between China and Russia and flows into the Sea of Okhotsk. Canoes of this shape were fast, steady in the wind and quiet when used for hunting waterfowl in the reedy waters of the Kootenay territory. Though covered with canvas and made with nails, this canoe was otherwise built in the traditional way. The thwarts were doubled back under the inwale and wrapped with root. The stringers were held in place by the pressure of the ribs. The ends were closed with two battens nailed together and the center bottom stringer, which protruded several inches, helped to protect the bow. A bark seating pad has been anchored with two extra ribs. The paddler sat on the bottom and paddled several strokes on one side and then the same on the other.

MM #**143** L: 43¼" W: 6⅜" D: 4½"

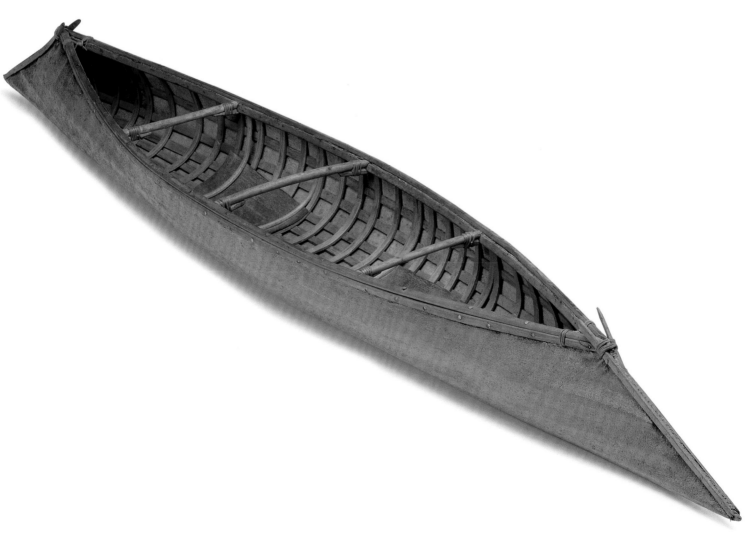

TOP: Kootenay Sturgeon-Nose Spruce Bark Canoe

Based on a Kootenay canoe in the Canadian Museum of Civilization and on a model made by Chief Eustan of the Kootenay. The sturgeon-nose canoes of North America were traditionally made from spruce or pine bark. The Kootenay variety had a strake of birchbark about the width of a hand between the gunwale and the spruce bark. The purpose of this was to prevent the spruce bark from ripping due to the pressure from the ribs. The birchbark was placed with the grain running longitudinally instead of the usual way so that it would act somewhat like a circuit breaker. If the ribs exerted too much pressure, the birchbark would rip, not the spruce bark, which was much harder to replace. The ends of the canoe were closed with three battens lashed together.

MM #**125** L: 43⅛" W: 6⅜" D: 4½"

BOTTOM: Lower Kootenay Sturgeon-Nose Spruce Bark Canoe

Based on a canoe from Washington state and on the writing of Dr. Otis T. Mason of the Smithsonian Institution. Adney built this model in 1927. Like the previous canoe, it had double gunwales, a strake of birchbark and three battens closing the ends. The thwarts were also doubled back and lashed in the same manner. The inside was quite different. A second layer of bark was lashed to floating ribs and then a second set of ribs and lashed stringers held the second layer of bark and floating ribs in place. This type of canoe was found in northern Montana, Idaho and Washington, as well as in British Columbia.

MM #**75** L: 44" W: 8⅜" D: 5⅜"

Lower Amur Birchbark Canoe

Based on drawings sent to Adney by Prof. Shinji Nishimura, Tokyo, in 1931. Adney built this model in 1933. This canoe from the Amur River, which forms the eastern border of China and Russia, was very similar in both shape and structure to the Kootenay and Shuswap canoes. As well, its floating decks, held only by the tight reverse curl of the birchbark, were identical to those of the Canadian Northwest, as were the stringers. Its bow and stern projections, extensions of the strong stems, were unique. There has been much speculation concerning their purpose. It is most likely that they were simply decorative. The other unique feature was the protective pieces of bark over the stems, which were sewn and gummed.

MM #**118** L: 33½" W: 5¼" D: 3½"

107

MIGRATION TO NORTH AMERICA

Adney was fascinated by the striking similarities between the birchbark canoes of the Amur region of Asia and the Kootenay–Shuswap canoes of lower British Columbia and the American Northwest. No other bark canoes in the world have their "sturgeon-nose" shape. He was too good a scholar to pronounce on the subject, but he was convinced that there were two plausible ocean routes from Asia to America that early peoples could have taken. The first, very obvious one is across the Bering Strait. Adney pointed out that the umiaks of northern Siberia and those of North America were virtually identical and easily capable of making the trip.

His second route linked the peoples of the Amur region with those of the Kootenay region. The Amur River drains into the Sea of Okhotsk. From there a boat route to America was plausible via Sakhalin Island (home of the Ainu), the Kurile Islands, the Kamchatka Peninsula, the Commander Islands and the Aleutian Islands. The Commander Islands are an extension of the Aleutian chain. Adney speculated that the crossing could have been accomplished in the very seaworthy baidarkas of Kamchatka, some of which held three people. Seventy years ago, Adney was one of the earliest scholars to argue that, from the Aleutians, Asians could then have come down the coast of British Columbia, existing mainly on the rich produce of the sea. During the last ice age, which lasted from roughly 30,000 BP (before present) to 12,000 BP, the Pacific Ocean was about 300 feet lower, thus exposing considerably more land between the continents. The theory, first expressed by archaeologists such as Knut Fladmark and David Kelley, that Asians first came to North America during the last ice age via an exposed coastal corridor in British Columbia has recently gained support, which in turn supports Adney's theory that the people of the Amur region could have reached the Kootenay area.

Goldi Birchbark Canoe

Based on a model in the Russian Imperial Museum, St. Petersburg, of a Goldi canoe of the lower Amur River, and on the studies of the Amur River canoes by Dr. Otis T. Mason of the Smithsonian Institution. The Goldi were a branch of the Tungus of eastern Asia, who lived on both sides of the Amur, in what is now China and Russia. This canoe was a more modern version of #118 (p.107), but with nailed gunwales, sheathing and thwarts mortised through both gunwales and pegged between the gunwales exactly in the manner of the Chipewyan.

The decks were also exactly the same as some found in the Canadian Northwest. The bark protectors over the stems were sewn with rawhide.

MM #**119** L: 37" W: 5⅝" D: 3⅞"

Tungus Birchbark Canoe

Based on a model in the Imperial Academy of Sciences, St. Petersburg, and on a report of the Smithsonian Institution, 1899. The Tungus (Evenk) lived on tributaries of the Amur River and on the lower Lena and Kolyma rivers, east of the Yakut. They were mainly reindeer herders, riding them with saddles and bridles, and lived in bark-covered teepees. The strange outwale was perhaps necessary since there were no stringers to give longitudinal strength to the canoe. The unique addition to the outwale also had the effect of forcing the inwale down, thus producing the sheer that was wanted. The stem protectors on these Amur canoes were not found in any North American canoes.

MM #**68** Length: 35½" W: 8¼" D: 4¼"

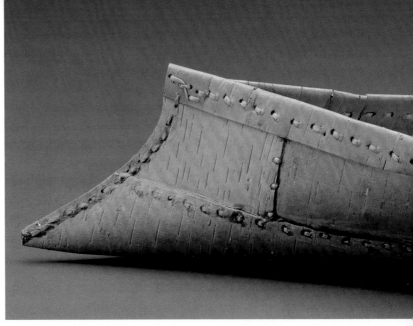

Yakut Birchbark Canoe

Based on a model in the Russian Imperial Museum, St. Petersburg, of a Yakut canoe from the lower Amur River, and on the work of Dr. Otis T. Mason. Adney built this model in 1932. The Yakut (Sakha) were subdued with great ferocity by the Cossacks in the seventeenth century, and in the 1650s they and the Tungus were almost wiped out by smallpox. They lived on the Lena River, northwest of the Amur. This model perhaps does not provide a full representation of the original canoe, since it has very little structural integrity. It has no gunwales and no stems, and the thwarts are just butted up against the gunwales and held by lashing underneath. Both this canoe and the previous one (#48) were very broad bottomed due to the join of the bark at the bilge.

MM #**48** L: 29¼" W: 6½" D: 4⅝"

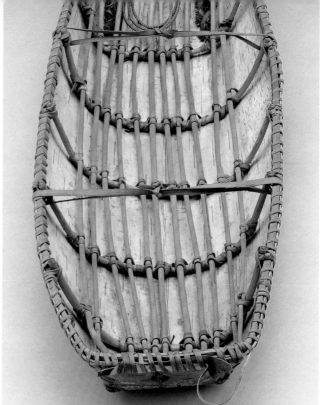

Ainu Birchbark Canoe

Based on a model at the Sapporo Museum, Hokkaido Imperial University, Japan, dated 1866. Adney built this punt-shaped model in 1933, based on the Ainu people of Yezo and Sakhalin Island, Japan. The Ainu were the original aboriginal people of Japan. This model represents the only known birchbark canoe built with the grain running longitudinally (except for #125, p. 106, built with a longitudinal birchbark strake). The model represents an eight-foot canoe, thus the circumference of the tree had to be at least eight feet. The bark was folded in the corners, which were stuffed with bog moss to keep out the water. The canoe had no stem, just stringers lashed to the ribs, which protruded above the gunwales. Since the grain ran longitudinally, it was important that the ribs be free to expand without pressure on the gunwales, which would cause the bark to rip. This temporary canoe was for a single paddler and was probably used to cross rivers.

MM #**102** L: 19" W: 5½" D: 3¼"

Ainu Bark Canoe

Based on a model given to the American Museum of Natural History, New York, by William Curtis James in 1998. The type of bark was unknown to Adney. The bark canoes of the Ainu are long extinct. The only known examples of their canoes are the two models that Adney reproduced. The bark appears to be too heavy and coarse to reverse. There are no stems or keelson, just single gunwales lashed with fiber and minimal stringers. The model appears unfinished. Did the Ainu make the voyage to America via the Commander-Aleutian islands route, as Adney suggested? Certainly not in the two Ainu canoes featured here!

MM #**156** L: 18" W: 7⅜" D: 4⅛"

Yukaghir Dugout Canoe

Based on a figure from the American Museum of Natural History. The canoe represents a poplar dugout of the Yukaghir people of the upper Kolyma River in northeast Siberia. The Kolyma is a major river flowing into the Arctic. Adney made very few dugout models. This is one of three at The Mariners' Museum. All three have been featured together, partly to make Adney's point that these Yukaghir dugouts not only closely resembled the shape of the Inuit kayak, but also that of the Athapascan bark canoe and dugout. The Yukaghir people were also one of the three Native groups of the Kamchatka Peninsula, which forms part of Adney's theoretical migration route to North America.

MM #**81** L: 42¾" W: 4½" D: 3¼"

Athapascan Dugout Canoe

Based on canoes from the upper Yukon River that Adney saw in 1898 in Dawson City. Adney made this model before 1928. He did not indicate the type of wood that the Athapascans used to make their dugouts. This canoe is somewhat similar both to Athapascan birchbark canoes and to the dugouts of northeastern Siberia.

MM #**104** L: 27³⁄₁₆" W: 3⅝" D: 3⅛"

Yukaghir Hunting Canoe

Based on a model in the American Museum of Natural History, New York. The canoe was made from three thin poplar boards, sewn together with sinew and gummed. This was the plank version of model #81. It would have been extremely light and easy to portage. The Yukaghir, once so numerous that their camp-fires resembled "the stars in the sky," were almost exterminated by 1800 as a result of disease and Russian aggression.

MM #**100** L: 39" W: 4¹³⁄₁₆" D: 3⁵⁄₈"

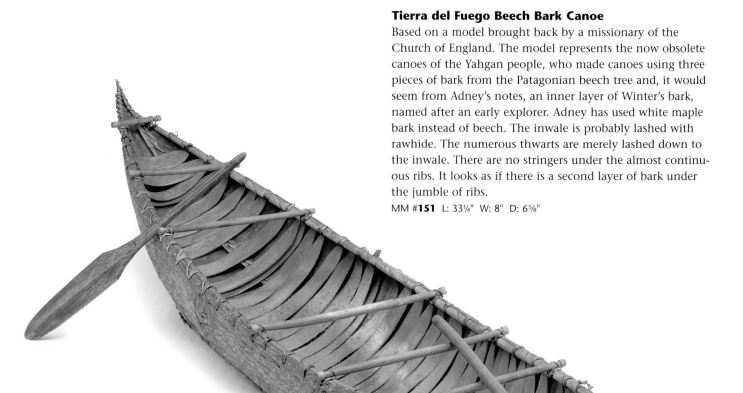

Tierra del Fuego Beech Bark Canoe

Based on a model brought back by a missionary of the Church of England. The model represents the now obsolete canoes of the Yahgan people, who made canoes using three pieces of bark from the Patagonian beech tree and, it would seem from Adney's notes, an inner layer of Winter's bark, named after an early explorer. Adney has used white maple bark instead of beech. The inwale is probably lashed with rawhide. The numerous thwarts are merely lashed down to the inwale. There are no stringers under the almost continuous ribs. It looks as if there is a second layer of bark under the jumble of ribs.

MM #**151** L: 33¼" W: 8" D: 6⅝"

Jamamadi Purple Heart Bark Canoe

Based on a model from the Alto Purus River, a southern tributary of the Amazon close to the eastern border of Peru, collected by J.B. Steele in 1901 and now at the Smithsonian Institution. Adney also based this model and the next two on the 1935 unpublished study of South American bark canoes by Commander Kendell Roop, USN. Purple heart trees are very large and the bark is probably too thick to reverse, as is done with elm and spruce bark. The thwarts were mortised through the bark and the ends lashed with fiber. The ends were raised by crimping the bark at the thwarts and then pulling it together to form a tube. The critical construction in this craft was the triangle formed by the thwarts and the first lashing at the end. There was great pressure on this lashing, which held the ends up, and the ends put strong pressure on the top edges of the bark in the mid-section. If the canoe was to carry a heavier load, the ends needed to be extended to keep the mid-section from sagging.

MM #**157** L: 29" W: 5½" D: 4½"

Woodskin Bark Canoe, Guyana

Based on a 13-foot canoe from the upper Essequibo River, Guyana (formerly British Guiana) and from information from the curator of the British Guiana Museum, Georgetown. This type of canoe was also used on the Rupununi and Mazaruni rivers. These canoes were usually made from a single sheet of purple heart (murianara) tree and sewn with bush rope. A wedge-shaped incision was made in the outer bark at the point of rise. The inner layer was folded on itself, thus keeping the canoe watertight. The seats were made from *ité* palm wood, held up by pegs sewn to the inwales, and the structure of the canoe was strengthened by inwale poles lashed to the bark. The elevation of the ends was maintained by fiber lashing across the wedge incision and by the natural curve of the inwale poles.

MM #**158** L: 30" W: 6⅝" D: 4½"

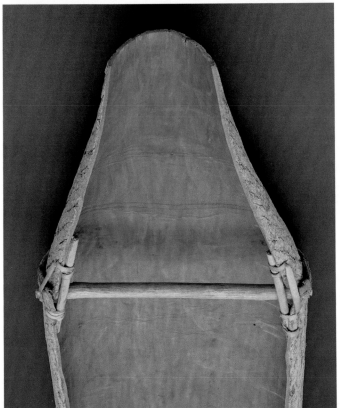

Woodskin Bark Canoe, Guyana

This model is a smaller version of the previous one (#158), but without any gunwale structure. The uprise at the ends was held in place by mortised thwarts with pegs lashed across the wedge incisions in the outer bark. It is hard to imagine a more primitive form of canoe. The ends would tend to droop and it is hard to imagine using this craft for any serious purpose. However, purple heart bark is very tough and does not curl, so this canoe may have been stronger than it appears. Adney classified the Amazon and Guyana bark canoes in a single grouping and pointed out the similarities in basic shape with the dugout canoes of the Carib and Seminole.

MM #**159** L: 26" W: 6" D: 2¾"

CANOES OF THE
Fur Trade

The upper half of North America is the only place on the planet where two things came together to produce a unique frontier history: abundant birchbark and an arterial system of rivers and lakes perfectly suited to form canoe routes across the continent. The map of the growth of the birch tree is virtually the map of Canada below the tree line. As Adney made so clear, no other bark could have been used to build the great voyaging canoes, capable of carrying 8,000 pounds of cargo and a crew of eight. These canoes were the basis of Canada's first industry, the fur trade, and they were vital to shaping her borders.

A unique relationship based on the commerce of the fur trade and facilitated by the birchbark canoe developed between Europeans and Native peoples, which depended on mutual benefit in trade, not dispossession of land. The relationship was enhanced by the extraordinary technology and functional elegance of the Native birchbark canoe, which changed not at all over 300 years, except for an increase in size and the addition of nails.

Six-Fathom Birchbark Fur Trade Canoe

Based on an Iroquois canoe built for the Hudson's Bay Company. The original was over 38 feet long (the longest known fur trade canoe was 40 feet long). A canoe of this size could carry 8,000 pounds of cargo, plus a crew of 8 to 12 paddlers. The Iroquois became voyageurs and major canoe builders for the fur trade after the amalgamation of the HBC and The Northwest Company in 1821. After this, many French-Canadians left for better paying jobs and their positions were filled by the Iroquois. The decoration on this canoe is typical of Iroquois builders, especially the white spirals and the rayed disks, a symbol of protection that went back to Dutch influence. These same disks can be found on

New England Dutch barns and on craft in the Dutch East Indies. The elaborate headboards are unusual, indicating that this canoe would have been used to carry senior officials of the fur trade. From the shadow, the canoe appears to be slightly hogged. When loaded, it would have leveled off, leaving a long bottom line. The Iroquois centered around Montreal built Algonquin-style fur-trade canoes. The curve of the ends was, to some degree, a builder's personal mark, but the rake of these ends represents one of the two major fur trade shapes. A canoe of this size could only be used on major waterways.

MM #**153** L: 92" W: 14½" D: 11¾"

Ottawa River Five-Fathom Birchbark Fur Trade Canoe

Based on a 30-foot Hudson's Bay Company canoe built by Algonquin builders at Lake Barrière and Grand Lake Victoria in the upper Ottawa River region in the 1890s. This area was one of the last to produce fur trade canoes. Adney built this model in 1929. The original canoe was built for Louis Christopherson for his personal use. He was very particular about the decoration that was put on his canoes. In this case, they were drawn by Amab Sarazin of Golden Lake and Maniwaki. They are typical of Algonquin figures. A canoe from 28 to 32 feet long was known as a *bâtard* (Bastard) canoe, because it was a hybrid, neither a North canoe nor a Montreal canoe. A canoe of this size was very versatile and could go places a Montreal canoe couldn't. It would have been paddled by a crew of six. The vertical stems and sharp rise of the gunwales were typical of the area, as well as in the region of lakes Abitibi and Kipawa. The pegged paddle guard *(barrage d'abord)* protecting the gunwale wrapping is unusual.

MM #**133** L: 73¼" W: 13⅛" D: 10⅛"

Hudson's Bay Canvas Fur Trade Canoe

Based on a 30-foot HBC canoe built at Lake Mistassini, Quebec, in 1930 by Cree builders. Similar canoes were also built by the Cree at Waswanipi, Quebec, into the twentieth century. Adney built this model in 1930. Although canvas, it is built exactly as a birchbark canoe would have been. Especially in the North, canvas began to replace bark by 1900, and this style of canoe is very similar to those of the Algonquins at Lake Barrière and Grand Lake Victoria. This model has the same vertical stems and long bottom as the previous model (#133). This canoe would have been paddled by a crew of six; in portaging, they carried it inverted with three men at each end. This is a purely functional canoe: the gunwales are nailed, the thwarts are notched, not mortised, and there is no external stem. This kind of canoe was usually 32 feet long.
MM #**127** L: 72" W: 13¼" D: 9⅛"

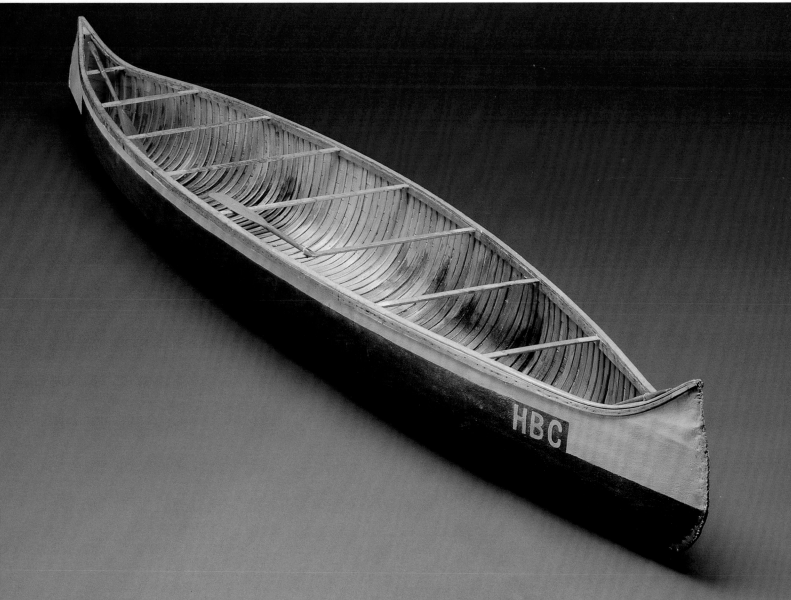

Five-Fathom Hudson's Bay Birchbark Fur Trade Canoe

Based on a 30-foot Express canoe *(canôt leger)* built for carrying senior officers of the Hudson's Bay Company in the mid-nineteenth century. In building this model, Adney used the paintings of Frances Ann Hopkins and a Native model collected by George M. Dawson of the Geological Survey of Canada in 1870. Adney built this model in 1928. It represents the kind of canoe used by Sir George Simpson, Governor of the Hudson's Bay Company, on his epic voyages across the continent. He usually had an elite crew of eight Mohawk paddlers and a guide. Many of their paddling times still remain unequaled. The canoe is shown with personal packs and Algonquin-style paddles. Seats are slung from the gunwales for passengers; the voyageurs sat on packs. The painted bow and stern circles are based on a 1901 Geological Survey of Canada photo of a Missinaibi fur trade canoe. A reinforcement strip of bark, painted blue, has been added under the gunwales; the roll-down seams in the bark at the ends are unusual and probably added for aesthetic effect. The bow shape is typical of the Bear Island, Lake Temagami, region.

MM #**120** L: 74" W: 12½" D: 5½"

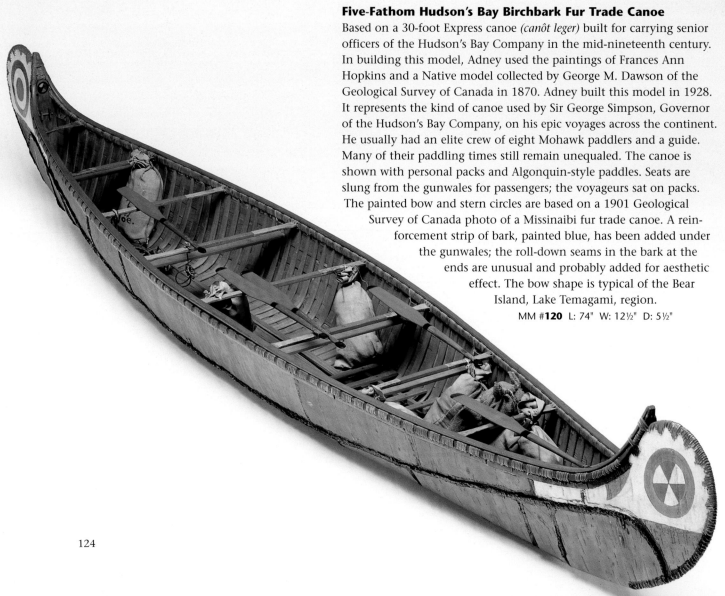

124

Têtes de Boule Four-Fathom Birchbark Fur Trade Canoe

Based on a model made by Chief Charles Pitiguay of Weymont, Quebec, on the St. Maurice River. Adney built this model in 1926. He called it a Nadoe Chiman (Iroquois canoe). It represents the fur-trade canoes that the Têtes de Boule of the upper St. Maurice River built for the Hudson's Bay Company. These canoes were quite different from their small canoes, which closely resembled the St. Francis Abenaki canoes. When Adney went to Weymont in 1926, he found that the Têtes de Boule had built about 200 canoes for the HBC. The bow and stern shapes are very similar to the Iroquois six-fathom canoe (#153, p. 121). The Iroquois, who were not good canoe builders before they migrated to the St. Lawrence region, put their mark on fur trade canoe building in the nineteenth century. Adney appears not to have gummed the seams of this canoe.
MM #**65**   L: 63¼" W: 12¼" D: 10¾"

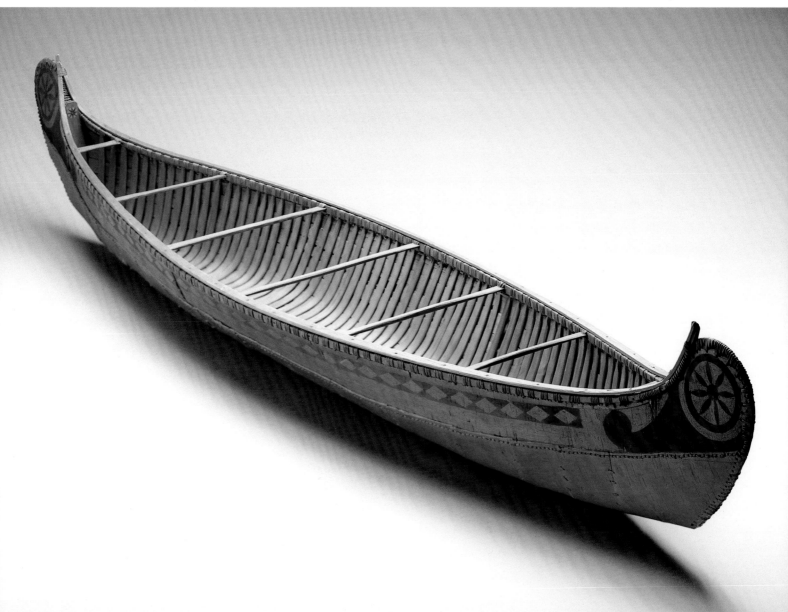

TOP: Ojibwa Three-and-a-Half-Fathom Birchbark Fur Trade Canoe

Based on a Bear Island, Temagami, "Long Nose" canoe, circa 1890, from a Canadian Pacific Railway photo. Adney built this model in 1925. The Ojibwa influence is clear in the sweep of the ends, an Ojibwa signature. The contrast with the bow of the other model below is striking. These canoes were built at the Bear Island HBC post into the 1890s. The shaped center thwart is puzzling. Usually this was done for portaging. This canoe seems too big for one man to portage (21 feet). Adney once saw an Ojibwa crew in a canoe like this paddle full speed into shore and, without slackening, jump out and beach the canoe with their arms under the thwarts.

MM #**129** L: 50⅝" W: 10¼" D: 8½"

BOTTOM: Three-Fathom Ottawa River Birchbark Express Canoe

Based on an Algonquin canoe built for Louis Christopherson in the 1890s at the HBC post at Grand Lake Victoria, Quebec. The shape of the bow and stern are very similar to #133 (p. 122). This canoe is a smaller version of the fur trade canoes used on the upper Ottawa River and the route to James Bay. The decoration was probably suggested by Christopherson. The gunwales and caps are nailed; lashing on the gunwales has been used only to secure the thwarts at the ends. These HBC canoes built in eastern Ontario and western Quebec were a critical link to the Algonquin canoe building that continues today at Maniwaki, Quebec, on the Gatineau River north of Ottawa.

MM #**89** L: 47¾" W: 9¾" D: 8¾"

Têtes de Boule Three-and-a-Half-Fathom Birchbark Fur Trade Canoe

Based on an Ojibwa-style Têtes de Boule canoe that Adney found at Grand Piles, Quebec, in 1925. The canoe was built by a Têtes de Boule builder on the upper St. Maurice River. Adney built this model in 1930. In his search for nineteenth-century fur trade canoes, this was practically the only one he found. He went to Grand Piles with great excitement, only to find this small and rather indifferent canoe, painted gray inside. The canoe is beamy and not very elegant, with rough planking and nailed thwarts. On the other hand, the paddles that he copied are beautiful examples of Têtes de Boule craftsmanship.

MM #**80**   L: 44¼"   W: 9¹⁄₁₆"   D: 8¼"

CANOE MODEL
Details

These pieces were made by Adney to illustrate the details of bark canoe construction.

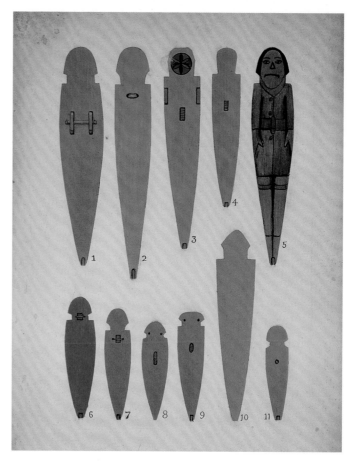

1 to 5 scale central area Ojibwa-type and Algonquin-type large and small headboards

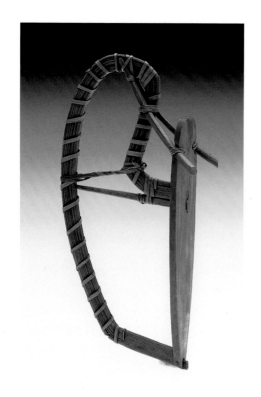

Algonquin fur trade stempiece

Algonquin fur trade stempiece

Iroquois old French-style stempiece

Ojibwa gunwale end lashing

Ojibwa ribs shaped, dried and ready to insert

Ojibwa gunwale end lashing

Maliseet ribs

Algonquin gunwale lashing

Montagnais (Innu) ribs

REPRINT OF AN ARTICLE FROM *HARPER'S YOUNG PEOPLE*, JULY 29, 1890

How an Indian Birch-Bark Canoe Is Made

by E.T. Adney

Peter Jo is an Indian (one of the Milicete tribe, who live in New Brunswick along the river St. John), and probably has spent the winter on snow-shoes in the woods chasing moose or caribou, now and then taking from his traps a fur-bearing sable or fisher. After the warm days of spring and early summer have thawed the frost out of the trees and ground, Peter begins to think of making another birch-bark canoe.

When he has finally determined to build Ug-we-d'n, he pulls from a large, straight, smooth canoe birch a sheet of thick bark, which is rolled up like a piece of carpet and laid aside.

The canoe is to be about 19 feet long all over, and 30 inches wide inside, so that if the tree is a small one, as is generally the case, a few extra pieces of bark must be peeled from other trees in order that the canoe bark may be pieced out at the sides or ends.

The wood-work is all split from the heart of a straight-grained white cedar log free from knots; except the cross-bars, which are of rock-maple. Long stringy spruce roots, peeled and split in half, or sometimes splints of basket ash, are used for sewing and lashing, a large awl being used to punch the holes through which they pass.

In a convenient spot a "bed," 20 feet long and 3 feet wide, is graded perfectly smooth and level, except that it may slope gradually toward both ends, being an inch or two higher in the middle.

The frame of the canoe resembles two bent "bows" held apart by five crossbars. These bows are each 16½ feet long, whittled square, with a bevel on the lower outside edge (Fig. 1), tapering toward the ends, which are notched as in Fig. 2. Mortises one-quarter inch wide are chiselled out to receive the ends of the cross-bars. Fig. 2 shows the shape and size of crossbars, and just where they belong. Each bar is slipped into place, and the ends of the "bows" are bent together, nailed, and tied with roots. They are held secure by small hard-wood pegs (Figs. 1 and 2), but are not lashed to the frame until afterward.

This frame is next laid exactly in the centre of the bed, and stout temporary stakes, 26 in number, and from 2 to 3 feet long, flat on one side, are driven perpendicularly into the ground close outside the frame at the places shown on lower side of Fig. 2. Three additional pairs of stakes, each pair an inch apart, as shown in Fig. 2, are driven into the ground beyond each end of the frame, so that the last pair are 9 feet from the middle crossbar. Each end of the frame rests upon a short post about 2 inches high (Fig. 3). Next each stake is pulled up, and laid close to the hole to which it belongs, and the frame is also laid aside. The bark is unrolled and spread out upon the bed, with white side up, and the frame is laid back, this time upon the bark, so that it will be in exactly the position occupied before. Short boards are laid across the frame, upon which heavy weights are placed, by which means the bark is held flat and perfectly immovable on the bed.

Next, all that part of the bark which extends beyond the sides of the frame must be bent up squarely or perpendicularly around the frame. But in order to do this, slits must be cut in the bark outwardly at right angles to the frame, and v-shaped gores taken out close to the end of each bar, and at points about half-way between. Figs. 3 and 4 show where these slits have been afterward sewed up. As the bark is bent up, each stake is driven back into the hole it occupied before. The tops of each opposite pair of stakes are now connected by a strip of cedar bark (see figures) which keeps them perpendicular.

It is now generally necessary to piece out the sides by strips of bark sewed with roots along the edges, as shown in Figs. 3 and 4 and illustration.

Twenty-eight pieces of cedar, 1 to 2 feet long and 1 inch wide, sharpened chisel-shaped at the end, are whittled out. In order to keep the bark from curling too far inward, the sharp end of one of these sticks (called an "inside stake") is slipped into the crack along the outer edge of the frame just opposite each outside stake, and the two are tied together near their upper ends. Carefully look at Fig. 5, and see how the bark is held perpendicularly between them. Long thin strips of wood are pushed in outside between the bark and the outside stakes (Fig. 3), and similar ones are put inside

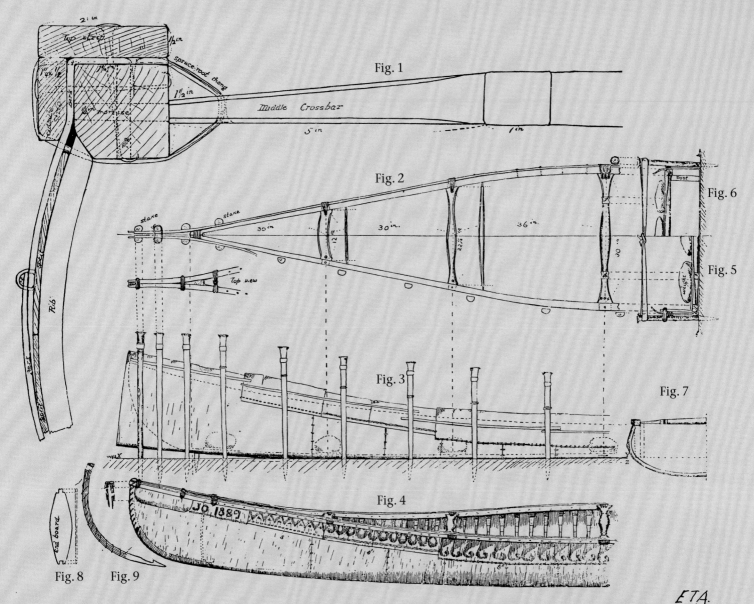

Fig. 1

Fig. 2

Fig. 6

Fig. 5

Fig. 3

Fig. 7

Fig. 4

Fig. 8   Fig. 9

E.T.A.

between the bark and the "inside stakes." Thus on all sides the bark is held perfectly straight up and down.

The weights are next removed, and the frame is carefully raised just high enough to allow a square post 7 or 8 inches long to be placed under each end of the middle crossbar. The weights are then put back upon that part of the frame. Similar posts, 9 inches high, are placed under each end of the next bar (of which there are two alike), and the weights replaced. Other posts, 12 inches long, are in the same way put underneath the shortest crossbar (of which there are two also). A single one, 16 or 17 inches high, is placed under each end of the frame. All the weights are replaced. Of course the lower ends of all these posts rest upon the bark, keeping it flat upon the bed as before; but the frame itself has assumed the curved shape seen in diagrams and illustration.

The temporary strips outside are taken away, and a long one — over 19 feet, 1 inch wide, and half an inch thick — put in place outside. This strip is bent to the same shape as the frame, and secured to it by slender nails that clinch on the inside. Thus the bark is held secure (Fig. 1). The crossbars are now lashed to the outer wood-work by roots that pass through holes in the bark and the ends of the bars, as in diagrams. The projecting edges of the bark are folded down and tacked to the frame, so as to offer a flat surface for the top strip that is put on afterward. The appearance at this stage is shown in the illustration on the following page.

The stakes are again pulled up, and the canoe is laid bottom upward upon two "saw-horses." It has now somewhat the appearance of a flat-bottomed double-

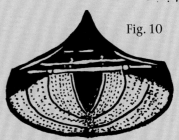

Fig. 10

pointed boat, for the beautiful shape of the finished birch canoe will not be taken until the ribs have been put inside.

With a pair of dividers, or by the eye alone, the curved line of the bow, shown in Fig. 3, is marked out, and the superfluous bark trimmed away with a knife. To stiffen the ends, a thin strip of cedar, over 3 feet long, 1 inch wide, and somewhat triangular, is split part way into about four strips, to facilitate bending; then bent with the thin edge outward, exactly as shown in Fig. 9 (so as to correspond with the curved line just marked out with the dividers), and wrapped tightly with a piece of twine. The purpose of the notch in the end of this stick will be explained later. This bent piece is placed between the edges of the bark. Both wood and bark are then sewed together by an over-and-over stitch, as in Fig. 4.

The canoe is next laid right side up on a grassy spot, and a pitch is prepared of rosin and grease melted together in a small pot, either one or the other being added in making, until the pitch will neither crack off in cold water nor melt too easily in the sun. Long strips of cloth are saturated with melted pitch, and pushed from inside into the cracks alongside the bow pieces that have just been sewed into place. The edges of the slits along the sides may now be sewed together, but that is not always done. Each crack is covered inside with a thin piece of birch bark pasted down with hot pitch. The canoe is now ready for the very thin "splits" of cedar that lie edge to edge, and extend from end to end. They cover the entire inner surface of the bark, and lie underneath and at right angles to the ribs, which are tightly driven in over them. They are one-eighth inch thick, 9 feet long, and as wide as they can conveniently be made. Their ends lap an inch or two where they meet in the middle of the canoe.

The ribs, about fifty in number, have been prepared of fresh-cut cedar, then steamed with hot water until pliant, then bent each to its proper shape, and laid away until perfectly dry and stiff. They are held in shape till dry by loops of cedar bark, which pass around outside. They should be bent two at a time, for a single rib is sure to break if bent alone. Each loop may hold several pairs of ribs, fitting one within another. Those intended for the middle portion of the canoe are 3 or 4 inches wide, while the end ones are narrower; but all are carefully whittled to a uniform thickness of a scant half-inch. The longest ones must be cut over 4 feet in length. It is at this stage that the greatest judgment is needed, inasmuch as the shape of the ribs determines the shape of the canoe, whether it is to be deep or shallow, rounded or comparatively flat on the bottom. Fig. 10 shows the shape of the principal ribs of an average canoe.

Commencing at the end, the space that each rib is to occupy is carefully measured with a splint of basket ash, and each rib (purposely cut a little longer than seems necessary) is tightly driven into place with a long stick and a mallet over the long thin "splits" that line the inside. Each rib, therefore, is driven into the exact place for which it had been shaped beforehand, and as the stiff ribs yield but little, the bark is forced out to the proper shape. Between the middle bar and the next there may be 10 ribs; between that and the shortest bar there may be 8 ribs, and between the shortest one and the end there may be 6 ribs — 48 in all.

Next, the bows are stuffed as full of shavings as possible, and the thin cedar boards (Figs. 8 and 10) are driven into place, the notch in the lower end fitting into the notch in the bow piece, shown in Fig. 9, and mentioned before.

Two long top strips half an inch thick, about 2 inches wide in the middle (Fig. 1), and 1 inch wide at ends, are nailed along the upper surface of the gunwales. These are the same length as the outside strips. The ends of the top and outside strips, which extend beyond the frame itself, are next to be securely bound together (see end of finished canoe) by roots that pass through the bark and around the four loose ends in the three places shown in the diagrams. But before that is done, the ends of these strips must be notched to fit the projecting end of the bow piece (diagrams). A piece of bark with rounded corners (Fig. 4) is also usually folded down over the upper edges of the bark underneath both side and top strips before they are lashed together.

Every crack and seam must now be stopped up with hot pitch plastered on outside with a small wooden paddle, and swathed down with the moistened finger. A piece of stout canvas, 4 inches wide and nearly 2 feet long, is pasted with pitch over the sewed edges of the bow, as shown in Fig. 4. Remember that pitch will not stick to a wet surface. It constantly happens in the practical use of a canoe on Canadian rivers that a large "eye hole" in the bark begins to let in the water, or a blow from a hidden rock chips the rosin from a crack or seam. A landing is then effected, the canoe is carefully lifted from the water, and laid upside down on a level place. By sucking with the mouth the leaky spot is soon found. With a torch of birch bark or drift-wood the bark is thoroughly dried about the leak, and the rosin where cracked is heated and pressed back

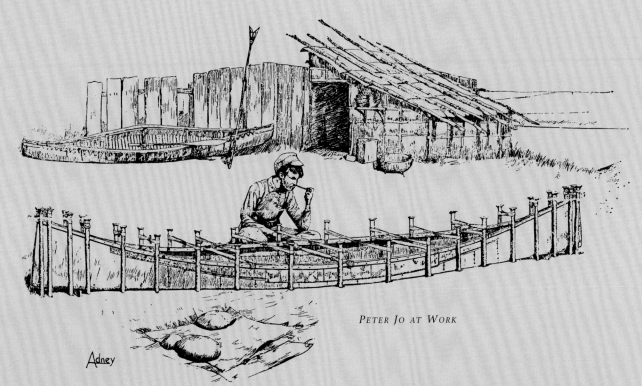

PETER JO AT WORK

Adney

in place, or fresh pitch is put over a newly made hole.

The curious decoration shown in Fig. 4 is sometimes painted, but is usually seen on such canoes as are made of the dark red-colored bark known as "winter bark," that has been peeled before the sap began to flow. This rough red surface must be moistened and scraped off, so as to expose the smooth yellow surface underneath, but enough is left to form the ornamental pattern, together with the date and maker's name, seen around the edge of the canoe.

In making such a canoe, every detail of the diagrams must be carefully studied. The section (Fig. 1) and also diagram of stitches are half-size. All the rest are drawn to a scale of one-half inch to the foot. Notice that in Fig. 2 several different stages are indicated in one diagram, which may lead to confusion, unless the text also is followed. Fig. 5 is one half of a section amidships showing how the bark is bent up outside the frame, and how the outside stakes are driven in place, and how the outside stake is tied to the small wedge-shaped "inside stake." Fig. 6 is the other half of the same section, and shows a later stage, with post underneath the crossbar, and Fig. 7 is the same section after ribs are in.

Canvas may be used instead of bark, but the cloth must be drawn up around the frame without cutting the slits necessary in the unyielding birch bark. I know a certain dark shiny canoe, made by a white man, that in a series of exciting races was more than a match for a dozen Indian birch canoes.

Where it is neither desirable nor practical to build a full-sized canoe, an interesting model may be made by following the diagrams closely. A board with gimlet-holes, into which the stakes are driven around the frame, may be used instead of a bed of earth. For sewing and tying, very fine splits of ash should be used instead of spruce roots. A model, built on a scale of one-sixth, would be about thirty-eight inches long, which experience has shown to be the smallest size to which every single proportion can conveniently be reduced. Such a one would be just three times the size of diagrams 2 to 10, and one-third the size of Fig. 1. A larger one would be made more easily. The Indians built pretty toy canoes, but insist that it is impossible to build a small one exactly as a large one is made — which is not true. It is always difficult to make anything properly, but perhaps there would be even more satisfaction in building a small canoe that would be a perfect model also, than in attempting a full-sized one.

Peter Jo thinks that the magic canoe of Hiawatha, so beautifully illustrated in the poem, must have been "sartin, very poor canoe" but perhaps we may excuse Mr. Longfellow when he wrote his charming poem for not having given a more minute description of the Cheemaun of the legendary Ojibway that

"floated on the river
Like a yellow leaf in autumn
Like a yellow water-lily."

133

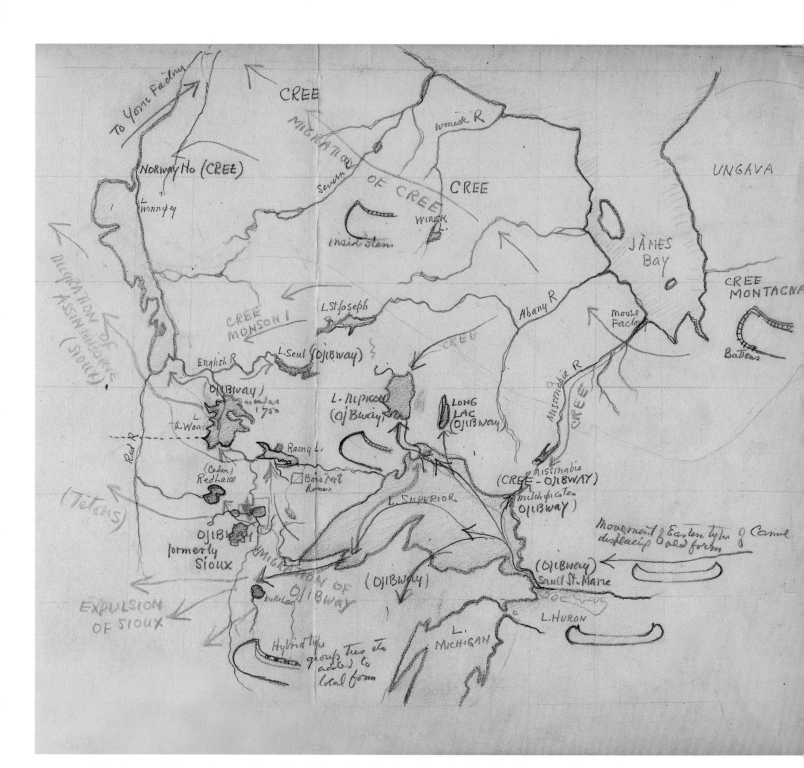

Adney's map of the western section of the Eastern Woodlands region, showing historic westward migrations of Native peoples and the subsequent diffusion of different canoe types.

The Birchbark Canoe

Tappan Adney's 63 years of research preserved a vital part of North America's Native heritage. It did the same for the history of early exploration and the fur trade. The history of the fur trade and exploration is well documented, but not that of the great voyaging canoes used by the traders and explorers. The landscape those hardy individuals traversed, the northern half of North America, is a land of rivers and lakes. Nowhere else in the world can be found such a vast arterial system of waterways.

The geography of this vast region was made for the canoe. As the eminent Canadian canoeist Bill Mason put it, God first created the canoe, and then the country to go with it. The predominant feature of this realm of the bark canoe is the Canadian Shield, which lies at the heart of Canada and comprises almost three-quarters of the nation's territory, from Labrador to the Rocky Mountains. It is a land of elemental and brooding beauty. In geological terms, the Shield is a massive bed of extremely hard rock into which agriculture intrudes only in small patches. Ninety-five percent of the area is beyond the reach of agriculture.

Except along the southern fringe of the Shield, this region was populated by hunter-gatherers. In the lands to the south, the three sisters — corn, beans and squash — augmented hunting, but on the Shield Native life centered on hunting, trapping and fishing along waterways. Summer trade between Native groups was also almost exclusively by canoe.

Indeed, it is impossible to imagine Native existence in northern North America without the canoe. Not only did it sustain life through hunting, fishing and trade, it was the means of gaining knowledge beyond the limits of a people's established territory and it maintained cultural identity by transporting fragmented hunting groups to the annual gathering places or to their communal winter camps. And, of course, the canoe was the central element in warfare, allowing a war party to travel over long distance at great speed.

Birch trees (*Betula alba*) inhabit northern latitudes around the globe. In North America the paper or canoe birch (*Betula papyrifera*) provides the best bark for canoe building, and a map of the North American range of the birch tree is essentially the map of the Canadian Shield, where the birchbark canoe reigned supreme on a continent-wide system of waterways.

Indigenous bark canoes existed in many parts of the world, but only in northern North America did they reach such perfection that they continued, even after European contact, to be the central feature of European expansion across the continent. Tappan Adney's papers record his exhaustive search for all forms of indigenous bark canoes. He identified eight bark canoe regions worldwide: North America; the Amur Valley of Siberia; Yezo Island, Japan; Australia and New Zealand; northern South America; Tierra del Fuego; the Congo region of Africa; and northern Europe in prehistoric times. As the latter two regions are tenuous, it is more realistic to put the number at six.

Adney made it clear in his writing that the presence of bark craft in prehistoric northern Europe was conjectural, based mainly on linguistic links between the words for bark and those for various watercraft. He speculated that the introduction of iron tools into Europe some thousands of years ago resulted in the end of the bark canoe era.

Outside North America, except for the bark canoes of the Amur Valley, indigenous bark canoes were uniformly primitive. The saucer-shaped eucalyptus canoe of Australia and the purple heart canoe of the Orinoco region of South America were both rudimentary. The same goes for the beech bark craft of Tierra del Fuego and the junk-like canoes of Japan's Ainu. The bark canoes of the Amur Valley were more sophisticated solely because they were fashioned from birchbark.

In North America, Native canoe builders used various types of bark: elm, spruce, ash, chestnut, oak, basswood, hickory, beech, cottonwood and birch. But, of all these bark types, and others around the world, only the bark of the birch tree allows sophisticated shaping. The explanation for this anomaly is deceptively simple. Worldwide, bark used for making canoes has a longitudinal grain; that is, the splitting grain runs lengthwise along the tree trunk. The single exception is the birch

Designs scraped in birchbark. The darker bark is the original winter bark. The bark around the design has been scraped through to the lighter layer beneath. These are Têtes de Boule designs from a large canoe at Waymont, Quebec.

tree, whose bark has a transverse grain that runs around the trunk's circumference. Bark with a longitudinal grain can only be crudely shaped, so canoes constructed from this type of bark shared basic characteristics. A long sheet of bark was stripped from the tree, shaped into a rough form with ribs, gunwales and thwarts, and then clamped at both ends in some way to keep the water out. The bark could not be cut transversely without compromising its strength.

The bark of the birch, by contrast, can be shaped to make a canoe of exquisite elegance. As the birchbark is laid out on the building bed, its lines run from gunwale to gunwale. Slits can be made along the length of the canoe, similar to the darts of a dressmaker, without compromising the bark's strength. Once these slits are sewn with spruce root and caulked with a mix of pine or spruce gum, charcoal and animal fat, each slit is as strong as any other part of the canoe. Moreover, birchbark does not shrink or expand even when wet, and it is highly resinous and thus resistant to rot.

Because of its unique properties, birchbark was a key commodity in Native cultures throughout the northern hemisphere. Besides being used in canoe building, it was employed in covering wigwams and for various containers. In parts of Asia it was used for purposes as disparate as roofing and shoes. For Native peoples fortunate enough to live in good birch country, such as the Canadian Maritimes and the St. Lawrence Valley, birchbark was also an important trade item, thus exerting its influence far beyond the natural boundaries of the birch tree.

In addition, birchbark was an important medium for art and the recording of Native heritage. If the bark is collected when sap is flowing freely, when the inner surface of the bark is exposed to air it soon acquires a reddish orange color that deepens with age to a rich purplish brown.

The inner bark becomes the outer surface of the canoe and, if the darker outer layer is scraped away, a lighter layer is revealed. By scraping selectively, figures, designs or symbols can be created on the canoe. Many Maliseet builders identified their canoes with a "dupskodigun," or signature of unscraped bark.

Within North America, Adney identified three distinct bark canoe regions: the eastern woodlands; the northern British Columbia/Mackenzie Basin/Yukon/Alaska region; and a region comprising lower British Columbia, upper Washington and Idaho.

The eastern woodlands region encompassed an enormous area, from the east coast of Canada and the northeastern United States to lands occupied by the western

Ojibwa women at Lac Seul, Michigan, in 1918, lashing the gunwales of a canoe. Women usually did the lashing and gumming of canoes.

Cree beyond Hudson Bay. The eastern woodland canoe had to be tough enough to navigate turbulent rivers, yet light enough to be easily portaged. It consisted of three layers: the bark, the ribs (which give the canoe its shape and strength) and a thin layer of sheathing between bark and ribs. The ribs and sheathing were usually made from northern white cedar, which, like birchbark, was light and resistant to rot. White cedar was another staple of Native life, being the wood of choice for toboggans, snowshoes, cradleboards and many other necessities.

The canoes of the Northwest (northern British Columbia/Mackenzie Basin/Yukon/Alaska) were of two types. One was similar in construction to the canoes of the eastern woodlands, and the other closely resembled the Inuit kayak: a rigid lattice frame covered with bark rather than skin. The difference in covering reflected usage; the Inuit kayak frame had to withstand heavy seas, while the inland kayak-type canoe of the Northwest had to be carried over long distances.

Craft built by canoeing peoples of the Northwest — Chipewyan, Slavey, Dogrib, Yellowknife, Gwich'in (Kutchin or Loucheux), Beaver, Hare, Tanana, Han, Tuchone,

Kaska, Secani, Tahltan and Wet'suwet'en (Carrier) — did exhibit local differences. Yet, because all these groups were somewhat isolated from the main stream of continental canoe traffic, the vessels they constructed typically retained their original characteristics.

Kayak-type canoes were used by peoples of the Barren Lands and woodland peoples who hunted into the Barren Lands. Hunters pursued game on foot; they needed a craft that could be easily carried for a hundred miles or more and then be used for crossing rivers. As one French missionary commented, "Part of the time it carries us, and part of the time we carry it." The frames were often made of white birch and, in the autumn, the canoes were sometimes dismantled and the frames used for snowshoes, arrows or spears.

The third North American canoe type, that of the Kootenay and interior Salish of lower British Columbia and the upper American Northwest, was unlike any other on the continent. Its unique shape was found only in one other place in the world, the Amur Valley of Siberia. This ram-ended (sturgeon-nosed) canoe sported a long nose that protruded forward and aft below the water line.

Forest rangers at Outlet Bay, Lake Temagami, in 1895. The
photograph shows an interesting range of canoe shapes.

It was made from a variety of bark types — birch, pine, spruce, fir or balsam. Its odd form was not suited to navigating rapids but did allow the canoe to be paddled effectively in a strong wind and on smooth water or in the many marshes of the region. The striking similarities between the Kootenay and Amur Valley canoes provide powerful evidence for the migration theories of scholars who argue that the western hemisphere was populated via the Bering Sea land bridge at the end of the last ice age, approximately 11,000 years ago.

Adney developed his own method of categorizing the Native canoeing peoples of eastern Canada and the United States based on distinctive aspects of canoe construction. These divisions, described in detail in *The Bark Canoes and Skin Boats of North America*, are important to Adney's overall view of Native bark craft and to his thesis about the central place of the birchbark canoe in the history of North America. Briefly, Adney divided Native bark canoe peoples into "inner" and "outer" categories, with outer representing older and more primitive peoples and inner more recent and advanced. The outer canoes were characterized by a single gunwale continuously wrapped (close-sewn) with root for the entire length of the gunwale, resulting in what Adney termed an "imperfect foothold." Inner canoes had gunwales in pairs and group wrapping of root, thus leaving room for the tapered ends of the ribs to be firmly wedged between the inner and outer gunwales, in the space between the wrappings. This form of construction made a stronger and, in Adney's view, superior canoe. Adney's division scheme was important to his argument that the inner type of birchbark canoe construction was eventually perfected to such a degree that, virtually unchanged, it became the explorer's and fur trader's vessel.

Adney stated categorically that no other craft in the world could match the performance of the birchbark canoe. Indeed, for the first 200 years after contact, Europeans made not the slightest change to the Native canoe except to enlarge it in the interests of trade. And while recognizing that the birchbark canoe was key to the successful development of the fur trade, he stressed that the canoe had actually played a much grander role. The birchbark canoe was integral to the whole early history of Canada, and to that of the Mississippi Valley as well.

Adney was certainly not the first writer to extol the extraordinary virtues of the birchbark canoe. But he was the first scholar to make an exhaustive study of virtually all indigenous bark craft around the world.

Therefore, he was uniquely positioned to make the following claim:

> The adoption by the white man of the Indian's birch bark canoe and his webbed snowshoe ... has no counterpart anywhere else in the world. So perfectly adapted and of such high order was the material culture of the Natives whom the white discoverers found inhabiting the continent, that they adopted it in toto ... The heavy clumsy European small vessels were utterly useless. Champlain writes of his journey to the Great Lakes: "There is no craft known to the European except the canoe of birch bark of the savage with which the journey to the Upper Country can be made ..."
>
> Of the canoes of no other part of the world can anything of this sort be said. The other bark canoes are most interesting examples of primitive human ingenuity and adaptations, but have no historical importance. Had Europeans found at the St. Lawrence any other one ... of the barks of other regions of the world, it had been a different story.

Vincent Mikans of the Algonquin Reserve at Golden Lake, Ontario, with a roll of birchbark for a hunting canoe, 1927. Mikans, born in 1827 at Oka, Ontario, is 100 years old in this photograph. At the time he was the oldest canoe builder at Golden Lake.

The Canoe Frontier

When Europeans arrived in North America, they found only one river on the eastern seaboard that gave easy access to the interior of the continent: the St. Lawrence. By pure luck, France began to colonize the St. Lawrence Valley at a time when the region was relatively empty. Some time between the visits of Jacques Cartier in the 1530s and Champlain's establishment of New France in the early 1600s, the Iroquois had vacated the area. Thus the arriving French were not dispossessing Native people and had the good sense to realize that the best economic opportunity in this vast land of forests and water was to be found in the trade in furs with their Native neighbors. Neither did the French covet new lands to the extent that other colonizing nations in the western hemisphere did. Instead, they were chiefly interested in reaping its bounty, and so French explorers quickly established trading relations with Native peoples based on highly ritualized diplomacy that recognized these groups as sovereign nations. The French quickly adopted Native protocol, as one record states, "participating in condolence ceremonies for the dead; smoking peace pipes; and even dancing in silk stockings and powdered wigs to the beat of the Native drums."

Initially, Native traders approached the French, sometimes in flotillas of a hundred or more birchbark canoes. Thus began the St. Lawrence trade fairs in the 1660s, a physical and cultural coming together of very different peoples, and a mingling of the traditions of medieval European fairs and the Native gathering places. By the mid-seventeenth century, the French began to use the canoes of Native allies to probe inland, driven by a desire to extend trade and by an intense curiosity about the possibility of a Northwest Passage to the Orient. When Champlain first ventured inland, he packed his Chinese robes for the ceremonial meeting he believed was imminent.

At first, French colonizers went as guests of their trading allies, who made it clear that a trading alliance was an all-encompassing relationship. Trading partners were expected to demonstrate generosity in the exchange of gifts and in military assistance; their enemies became your enemies. The French had no alternative but to accept these terms if they wished to trade. The result was a century of warfare with their allies' enemies, the Iroquois, who on several occasions came close to annihilating New France.

Against a backdrop of intermittent warfare with the Iroquois, the trading relationship itself was surprisingly

Adney's sketch of a 1752 thirty-six-foot French fur-trade canoe with nine thwarts. The drawing shows a typical crew of eight voyageurs with the bourgeois sitting in the middle. The short, narrow Algonquin-style paddles of the voyageurs were much smaller than the long steering paddles of the bow and stern paddlers.

peaceful and increasingly defined the colony of New France. As the French moved inland in their bark canoes, they were astute enough to ask permission to establish trading posts on Native land.

By the beginning of the eighteenth century the French had established a vast trading empire that was centered on the Mississippi Valley, based on Native alliances, and made possible by the birchbark canoe. By 1701, the French had established two key points of control: Fort Pontchartrain (Detroit), which controlled Lake Erie and Lake Huron and the river routes south into Ohio territory, and Michilimacinac, at the junction of lakes Huron, Michigan and Superior. These two forts effectively gave the French canoe empire control of the trans-Appalachian West. From Michilimacinac, canoe brigades from Montreal could take either the northern route via Lake Superior to Grand Portage (later Fort William) or the southern route via the Chicago portage at the foot of Lake Michigan to the Illinois River and from there to the Mississippi. Altogether, the French had six canoe routes from the Great Lakes to the Mississippi. In effect, these canoe routes and Native trading alliances gave the French control of the interior of the North American continent.

As trade expanded, the French began establishing canoe-building centers along the St. Lawrence River, usually near Native communities. Native builders continued to do most of the construction, the men taking charge of the basic building and the women and children sewing spruce root and gumming seams. In 1632, with the establishment of Trois-Rivières as the major canoe-building center in New France, the construction of voyaging canoes became a major focal point of the colony's economy. As the building of birchbark voyaging canoes became standardized, three basic sizes emerged: the 36-foot *canot du maître* (Montreal canoe), the 26-foot *canot du nord* (North canoe), and a less well-known category, the *bâtard* (Bastard canoe), which ranged from 28 to 32 feet in length. The Montreal canoe, which could carry 8,000 pounds of cargo plus paddlers, was used on the routes from Montreal to the western end of Lake Superior and on the route to Michilimacinac and down the Mississippi. These great canoes are usually thought of as fur trade canoes, but may be better described as "voyaging canoes." They were the principal mode of transportation in northern North America and, beyond their role in the fur trade, were also used for exploration, diplomacy, war and religious proselytizing.

French missionaries played a vital role on the canoe frontier. Their tally of Native converts was low, but their presence was a reminder that treating Native people badly imperiled the immortal souls of the transgressors. French voyageurs generally heeded the message, which was backed up in New France by the all-encompassing power of the Crown.

Through the canoe trade, the birchbark alliance of the French and Native peoples developed into a "middle ground" of mutual accommodation. This relationship was most dramatically demonstrated in the Great Peace of 1701, a treaty signed at Montreal by French representatives and 1,300 Native delegates representing 39 Native nations. Journeying from as far away as Acadia, James Bay and the lands beyond the Great Lakes, the delegates all descended on Montreal in bark canoes. This moment marked a major event in North American history, for it represented the overwhelming effectiveness of the Native–French canoe-based trade alliances. The Great Peace represented the opposite of the mutual incomprehension that has characterized most encounters between indigenous peoples and colonizers throughout the world's history.

The nations of the Iroquois Confederacy, finally humbled by the Native–French trading alliance, were among the signatories to the Great Peace. Their agreement marked the end of the Iroquois threat to New France and also gave the French new freedom to exploit canoe routes from Acadia on the Atlantic to the Mississippi and beyond, and from James Bay in the north to the Missouri River in

the south. The Iroquois who would later move north to form communities around Montreal would become some of the foremost builders of voyaging canoes and some of the best voyageurs as well.

In the 1880s the development of railroads in Canada marked the end of the southern Canadian canoe frontier. In the North, however, the bark canoe continued into the twentieth century. The Hudson's Bay Company and the Geological Survey of Canada continued to use some birchbark canoes in the decades before World War One, and photographs of Native people in bark canoes in northern Canada in the 1920s, and occasionally later, are not uncommon. By the early decades of the twentieth century, photographs taken in the mid- and high North show the mingling of bark canoes and the new cedar-strip and cedar/canvas canoes of Peterborough and Fredericton. Pockets of birchbark building persisted, as at Maniwaki, north of Ottawa. But this was specialty construction for a few sportsmen and canoe addicts. By the beginning of World War One, the birchbark canoe as a working craft was essentially dead.

Though Adney mourned the passing of a great canoe-building tradition, he believed that this tradition was finding new life in the "carpentered" factory canoes of the Peterborough region of Ontario and the cedar/canvas canoes of Maine and, later, Fredericton, New Brunswick. Of this renaissance he would write:

> Unequalled for beauty of line and general all around utility, the Eastern woodlands canoe, and in particular the canoe of the eastern central or Abenaki group (Têtes de Boule, St. Francis-Kennebec-Maliseet) became the form of the modern factory-built canvas canoe, which it is interesting to note seems to have been first constructed by Indians of the Passamaquoddy division of the Maliseets, and a little later to be taken up under the direction of white men at Old Town on the Penobscot, Maine.

By the time Adney died, his beloved models had left the land that inspired them and his long-planned canoe book was unwritten. The bark canoe itself was only a memory; by 1950 the art of bark canoe building seemed to have virtually disappeared. Adney could not know that *The Bark Canoes and Skin Boats of North America*, based on his preliminary manuscript and notes, would indeed be published and that it would inspire a new generation of bark canoe builders and a revival of interest among scholars.

142

LEFT AND BELOW: Decorations on fur trade canoes became common in the latter period of the trade. According to Adney, many of the designs for these decorations first appeared in the 1820s, when the Hudson's Bay Company began employing Iroquois canoe builders. The Iroquois had not been known for constructing canoes, but when they migrated to the Montreal area in the eighteenth and nineteenth centuries they became among the best builders and voyageurs. Adney identified five basic designs on later fur-trade canoes, of which the rayed disk with four, six or eight points was the most common.

RIGHT: Adney claimed that the most common symbol painted on the bow and stern of Iroquois fur trade canoes was probably borrowed from Dutch traders of Albany, New York, who had extensive trading relations with Iroquois of the Mohawk and Hudson rivers. Adney observed the symbol, a six-rayed disk on a white background, on a Dutch East Indian sampan at the Mariners' Museum; it appears on New England Dutch barns as well as in the Dutch East Indies. The Iroquois typically also used traditional Dutch colors — red, blue and white — when painting the decoration. The six-rayed disk originated as the protective symbol of Hecate, the Greek goddess of witchcraft, and was designed to ward off witches, goblins and satyrs. The distinctive disk is also common in the Middle East and Europe; Adney observed it in the floor of Westminster Abbey.

Foxe Channel

Hudson Strait

Ungava Bay

George River

Fort Chimo

Naskaupi R.

Koksoak River

Caniapiscau R.

Michikamau Lake

Hamilton River

Hudson Bay

Great Whale River

Fort George River

Fort George

Big River

Gulf of

St. Lawrence

James Bay

Eastmain House

Eastmain River

Rupert R.

Fort Albany

Moose Factory

Rupert's House

Nottaway R.

Tadoussac

Saguenay R.

Fort Hope

Albany River

Missinaibi River

Abitibi R.

Harricanaw R.

St Maurice R.

Quebec

Lake Nipigon

Fort Abitibi

Trois Riviéres

Fort William

Fort Timiskaming

Ottawa

Montreal

St. Lawrence River

Portage

Michipicoten

Lake Superior

Mattawa River

River

Sault Ste Marie

Georgian Bay

Fort Frontenac

Fort Ticonderoga

Hudson River

Fort De Buade

Lake Huron

Michilimackinac

Fort Rouille (Toronto)

Lake Ontario

Wisconsin River

te

Lake Michigan

Fort Niagara (Conti)

Mohawk R.

Prairie Chien

Fort La Baye

Fox River

Fort Pontchartrain (Detroit)

Lake Erie

Fort Presque Isle

Fort la Boeuf

Allegheny River

nois

Chicago Portage

Fort Ouiatenon

Fort Sandusky

Fort Machault

Fort Duquesne (Pittsburg)

udreuil

Illinois River

Fort St. Louis

Fort Miami

Wabash River

Fort Pimitoui

Fort Crévecoeur

Fort Vincennes

Ohio River

Fort Orleans

St. Louis

Fort de Chartres

Kaskaskia

Fort Massiac

River

River

Tennessee River

Major Canoe Routes and Selected Forts of The Fur Trade Frontier

1600–1850

145

Glossary

AFT Towards the stern of a boat.

AMIDSHIPS The middle of a boat.

BASTARD CANOE Thirty-foot birchbark canoe used in the fur trade, from the French *canot bâtard*.

BATTEN Strip of wood or metal used to cover a joint between two planks.

BEAM The maximum width of a boat.

BILGE The inside of a boat's hull where the bottom turns into the sides, often referred to as the "turn of the bilge."

BOWLINE The curve of the bow of a boat.

BUILDING BED A bed of compacted earth, usually raised, but sometimes dug into the ground, where bark is laid out and held with stakes so it can be sewn together and then lashed to the frame to make a bark canoe.

CANOT BÂTARD Thirty-foot birchbark canoe used in the fur trade, known in English as the Bastard canoe.

CANOT DU MAÎTRE Thirty-six-foot birchbark Montreal canoe, used in the fur trade.

CANOT DU NORD Twenty-six-foot birchbark North canoe, used in the fur trade.

CAP STRIP Thin strip of wood fitted over the gunwale of a boat, also known as a gunwale cap.

CARRYBOARD Board attached to the middle crossbar of a canoe, sometimes used with a tumpline by the Mi'kmaq and Maliseet to distribute the weight when carrying a canoe.

CHINE A longitudinal line of transition between hull surfaces, such as where the bottom meets the sides.

CORACLE Small boat made of wickerwork covered with watertight material, used in Ireland and Wales.

CROOKED CANOE Birchbark canoe built by Eastern Cree with extreme rocker designed to negotiate rapids.

CROOKED KNIFE Drawknife with bent handle used by Native birchbark canoe builders.

CROSSBAR Horizontal bar between gunwales on a canoe. Also called thwart.

CUTWATER The forward edge of a boat's bow that divides the water.

DUPSKODEGUN Private mark or symbol of canoe maker.

FIRESTEEL Fiddlehead pattern joined at center by cross.

FLARE The upward and outward curve of a boat's side.

FLOATING DECK Birchbark deck fastened to the canoe only by the curl of the birchbark over the gunwales.

FORE Towards the bow of a boat.

GORES Slits pierced in building material (such as birchbark or walrus hide) so pieces can be sewn together.

GUNWALE Rail running along the sheer line of a boat, used to stiffen and protect the edge of the hull.

HALYARD Rope used for lowering or raising a sail on a boat.

HEADBOARD A piece of wood inserted near the ends of the canoe in the shape of the cross-section of the canoe, whose purpose is to strengthen the stempiece and ensure that the ends maintain their shape.

HEEL Stern end of a boat's keel and the lower end of the sternpost, to which the keel is connected.

HULL The body or frame of a boat.

INWALE The inboard component of a gunwale.

KEELSON Strip of wood that forms the backbone of the canoe, used for longitudinal stiffness on a canoe inside the hull when an external keel is undesirable.

LATH Thin, flat strip of wood, often used as in a series to form a framework.

MONTREAL CANOE Thirty-six-foot birchbark canoe used in the fur trade, also known as *canot du maître*.

MORTISE Hole or notch in a piece of wood designed to receive the end of another part, such as a tenon.

NORTH CANOE Twenty-six-foot birchbark used in the fur trade, also known as *canot du nord*.

OUTWALE Outer component of a gunwale.

RIB Piece of wood used transversely in a boat's hull.

ROCKER The curve of the bottom of the boat, seen from the side.

SHEATHING Thin strips of wood, usually cedar, that line the inside of many bark canoes and are held in place by the ribs.

SHEER The upward curve of a boat's lines from bow to stern.

STEM Upright piece of wood in the bow.

STRINGER Longitudinal structural member.

THWART Structural member extending across a canoe that supports the gunwale structure.

TUMBLEHOME On a boat with a rounded hull, tumblehome refers to the inward sloping of the upper part of its sides. It is also called "falling home."

TUMPLINE Sling for carrying a load (e.g., a canoe) on a person's back with a strap that fits around the forehead.

WULEGESSIS Flap of bark that protects the gunwale end lashings.

Sources

PICTURES

All color photographs of Tappan Adney canoe models in this book, as well as photographs of associated objects and decorations, are the property of and copyrighted by The Mariners' Museum. All of Adney's drawings that are reproduced here are from the Edwin Tappan Adney Collection, MS20, The Library at The Mariners' Museum, Newport News, Virginia, unless otherwise noted. All photographs, unless otherwise noted, are from the Edwin Tappan Adney Collection, MS20, The Library at The Mariners' Museum, Newport News, Virginia.

Credits

p. 10   Tappan Adney, Alaska 1901. From an advertising brochure for the J.B. Pond Lyceum Bureau of New York, 1904. Courtesy of Joan Adney Dragon.

p. 14   Lithograph by Tappan Adney for *St. Nicholas* magazine, a children's magazine published between 1879 and 1939, that featured English and American illustrators and writers.

p. 21   Lionel Judah, photograph by Tappan Adney.

p. 23   Athapascan pencil sketch, photograph courtesy of Peabody Essex Museum, #E-7, Folio 1, Neg #32,405.

p. 25   Tappan Adney, 1901. Painting by Edwin B. Child. Courtesy of Joan Adney Dragon.

p. 26   Tappan Adney, Provincial Archives of New Brunswick, Miscellaneous Collection P37-408.

p. 137   Ojibwa women at Lac Seul, Michigan, 1918. © Canadian Museum of Civilization, photographer Frederick Waugh, neg. #36729.

p. 138   Forest Rangers, Lake Temagami, 1895. Canadian Pacific Railway Archives NS1178.

QUOTES

All Adney quotes unless otherwise noted are from the Adney reference material at the Mariners' Museum, the McCord Museum, and the Canadian Museum of Civilization.

MUSEUMS

When Adney was doing his canoe research, Canada's national museum at Ottawa, the Canadian Museum of Civilization, was known as the Victoria Museum. In Montreal, Adney's association was with the McGill University Ethnological Museum. In the 1930s, that museum was closed. It is now part of the rejuvenated McCord Museum. For simplicity, the current names of these two museums have been used. The photos from the Geological Survey of Canada are now housed at the National Archives of Canada.

Adney's notes on the sources for his models are not systematic. The numbers for museum craft and models that Adney copied have been included where possible, but in many cases the numbers were not found.

Museum Abbreviations

AMNH   American Museum of Natural History, New York
CMC   Canadian Museum of Civilization, Ottawa
GSC   Geological Survey of Canada:
MM   Mariners' Museum, Newport News, Virginia
PMAE   Peabody Museum of Archeology and Ethnology, Harvard University
McM   McCord Museum, Montreal

Museum Reference Numbers

p. 43   Passamaquoddy Birchbark River Canoe, PMAE: 7128

p. 53   Modified Abenaki Birchbark Canoe, CMC: L 44

p. 65   Eastern Ojibwa Birchbark Canoe, PMAE, William Kimball Collection: 52975

p. 67   Eastern Ojibwa Birchbark Canoe, Canadian Pacific Railway, Photo 7870

p. 67   Eastern Ojibwa Birchbark Canoe, PMAE: 102121

p. 68   Montagnais Birchbark Canoe, CMC: III C 73

p. 69   Montagnais Birchbark Canoe, PMAE: 62490

p. 70   Naskapi Canvas Crooked Canoe, GSC: Photo 54533

p. 71   Naskapi Canvas Crooked Canoe, GSC: Photo 1823

p. 72   Eastern Cree Canvas Canoe, GSC: Photo III D 47

p. 86   Chipewyan Birchbark Canoe, CMC: VI A 18

p. 87   Chipewyan Birchbark Canoe, CMC: VI A 94

p. 88   Chipewyan Birchbark Canoe, CMC: VI A I B

p. 90   Dogrib Birchbark Canoe, CMC: VI C 15 Decoration, CMC: C 113

p. 91   Dogrib Birchbark Canoe, CMC: VI C 118, VI C 119

p. 98   Athapascan Birchbark Canoe, PMAE: 65446

p. 101   Athapascan Birchbark Canoe, McM: 2978

p. 114   Yukaghir Dugout Canoe, AMNH: Jochelson, *Memoirs*, XIII, 1900, Picture #42

Bibliography

Adney, Edwin Tappan. "The Building of a Birch Canoe." *Outing*, May 1900.

———. "How an Indian Birch-bark Canoe is Made." *Harper's Young People*. Supplement, July 29, 1890.

———. *The Klondike Stampede*. Vancouver: University of British Columbia Press, 1994.

———. "Moose Hunting with the Trochutin." *Harper's Magazine*, 1897–98.

———. "The Passing of the North Canoe." *Outing*, October 1902.

Adney, Edwin Tappan, and Howard I. Chapelle. *The Bark Canoes and Skin Boats of North America*. Washington: Smithsonian Institution Press, 1964.

Allen, Robert S. *His Majesty's Indian Allies: British Indian Policy in the Defence of Canada, 1774–1815*. Toronto: Dundurn Press, 1993.

Beardy, Flora, and Robert Coutts, eds. *Voices from Hudson Bay: Cree Stories from York Factory*. Montreal: McGill–Queen's University Press, 1996.

Belyea, Barbara, ed. *Columbia Journals: David Thompson*. Montreal: McGill–Queen's University Press, 1994.

Biggar, H.P., ed. *The Works of Samuel de Champlain*. Toronto: Champlain Society, 1922.

Brody, Hugh. *The Other Side of Eden: Hunters, Farmers and the Shaping of the World*. Vancouver: Douglas and McIntyre, 2000.

Bumsted, J.M. *Fur Trade Wars: The Founding of Western Canada*. Winnipeg: Great Plains Publications, 1999.

Burpee, Lawrence J., ed. *The Journals and Letters of Pierre Gaultier de Varennes de la Vérendrye and His Sons*. Toronto: Champlain Society, 1927.

Campbell, Marjorie Wilkins. *The Nor' Westers*. Toronto: Macmillan, 1974.

Diamond, Jared. *Guns, Germs and Steel*. New York: Norton, 1997.

Dickason, Olive. *Canada's First Nations*. Toronto: McClelland and Stewart, 1992.

Eccles, W.J. *The Canadian Frontier, 1534–1760*. Albuquerque: University of New Mexico Press, 1974.

Fladmark, Knut R. *The Feasibility of the Northwest Coast as a Migration Route for Early Man*. In *Early Man in America*, edited by Alan Lyle Bryan. University of Alberta Department of Anthropology Occasional Papers. Edmonton: University of Alberta, 1978.

———. *Times and Places: Environmental Correlates in Mid-to-Late Wisconsinan Human Population Expansion in North America*. In *Early Man in the New World*, edited by Richard Shutler, Jr. London: Sage, 1983.

Francis, Daniel, and Toby Morantz. *Partners in Furs: A History of the Fur Trade in Eastern James Bay, 1600–1870*. Montreal: McGill–Queen's University Press, 1983.

Franquet, Louis. *Voyages et memoires sur la Canada*. Quebec: *Institut canadien de Québec*, 1889.

Galbraith, J.S. *The Little Emperor*. Toronto: Macmillan, 1976.

Gidmark, David. *Birchbark Canoe*. Burnstown, Ontario: General Store Publishing Company, 1989.

———. *Birchbark Canoe: Living Among the Algonquin*. Toronto: Firefly Books, 1997.

———. *Building a Birchbark Canoe: The Algonquin Wabanaki Tciman*. Mechanicsburg, Pennsylvania: Stackpole Books, 1994.

———. *The Indian Crafts of William and Mary Commanda*. Mechanicsburg, PA: Stackpole Books, 1995.

Gilman, Carolyn. *Where Two Worlds Meet: The Great Lakes Fur Trade*. St. Paul: Minnesota Historical Society, 1982.

Gough, Barry. *First Across the Continent: Sir Alexander Mackenzie*. Toronto: McClelland and Stewart, 1997.

Harmon, Daniel Williams. *Sixteen Years in Indian Country: The Journal of Daniel Williams Harmon*. Toronto: Macmillan, 1957.

Havard, Gilles. *The Great Peace of 1701: French–Native Diplomacy in the Seventeenth Century*. Montreal: McGill–Queen's University Press, 1997.

Hayes, Derek. *First Crossing: Alexander Mackenzie, His Expedition Across North America, and the Opening of the Continent*. Vancouver: Douglas and McIntyre, 2001.

Hearne, Samuel. *A Journey from Prince of Wales's Fort in Hudson's Bay to the Northern Ocean, 1769, 1770, 1771, 1772*, ed. Richard Glover. Toronto: Macmillan, 1958.

Houston, C. Stuart. *To the Arctic by Canoe, 1819–1821: The Journal and Paintings of Robert Hood*. Montreal: McGill–Queen's University Press/Arctic Institute of North America, 1974.

Huck, Barbara. *Exploring the Fur Trade Routes of North America*. Winnipeg: Heartland, 2000.

Jaenen, Cornelius. *Friend and Foe: Aspects of French-Amerindian Cultural Contact in the Sixteenth and Seventeenth Centuries*. Toronto: McClelland and Stewart, 1976.

James, William W. *A Fur Trader's Photographs: A.A. Chesterfield in the District of Ungava, 1901–4*. Montreal: McGill–Queen's University Press, 1985.

Jauvin, Serge. *Aitnanu (the Montagnais Innu)*. Ottawa: Canadian Museum of Civilization, 1993.

Jenish, D'Arcy. *Epic Wanderer: David Thompson and the Mapping of the Canadian West*. Toronto: Doubleday Canada, 2003.

Jennings, John. *The Canoe: A Living Tradition*. Toronto: Firefly Books, 2002.

Karamanski, Theodore J. *Fur Trade and Exploration: Opening the Far Northwest, 1821–1852*. Vancouver: University of British Columbia Press, 1983.

Kent, Timothy. *Birchbark Canoes of the Fur Trade*. Ossineke, Michigan: Silver Fox Enterprises, 1997.

———. *Tahquamenon Tales*. Ossineke, Michigan: Silver Fox Enterprises, 1998.

Kohl, Johann Georg. *Kitchi-Gami: Life Among the Lake Superior Ojibway*. St. Paul: Minnesota Historical Society Press, 1985.

Koppel, Tom. *Lost World: Rewriting Prehistory—How New Science Is Tracing America's Ice Age Mariners*. New York: Atria Books, 2003.

Lahontan, Louis-Armand, Baron de. *New Voyages to North America*. Chicago: A.C. McClurg, 1905.

MacGregor, J.G. *Peter Fidler, Canada's Forgotten Explorer, 1769–1822*. Calgary: Fifth House, 1966.

Mackenzie, Alexander. *Voyages from Montreal on the River St. Laurence Through the Continent of North America to the Frozen Sea and Pacific Oceans in the Years 1789 and 1793*. Edmonton: Hurtig, 1971.

Mackie, Richard S. *Trading Beyond the Mountains: The British Fur Trade on the Pacific*. Vancouver: University of British Columbia Press, 1997.

McPhee, John, *The Survival of the Bark Canoe*. New York: Farrar, Straus and Giroux, 1975.

Mitchell, Elaine A. *Fort Timiskaming and the Fur Trade*. Toronto: University of Toronto Press, 1977.

Morrison, Jean, *Superior Rendezvous-Place: Fort William in the Canadian Fur Trade*. Toronto: Natural Heritage Books, 2001.

Nisbet, Jack. *Sources of the River: Tracking David Thompson Across Western North America*. Seattle: Sasquatch Books, 1994.

Norall, Frank. *Bourgmont: Explorer of the Missouri, 1698–1725*. Edmonton: University of Alberta Press, 1988.

Nute, Grace Lee. *The Voyageurs*. St. Paul: Minnesota Historical Society, 1955.

Parker, James. *Emporium of the North: Fort Chipewyan and the Fur Trade to 1835*. Regina: Canadian Plains Research Center, 1987.

Peers, Laura. *The Ojibwa of Western Canada, 1780–1870*. Winnipeg: University of Manitoba Press, 1994.

Peterson, Jacqueline, and Jennifer S.H. Brown, eds. *The New Peoples: Being and Becoming Metis in North America*. Winnipeg: University of Manitoba Press, 1985.

Pope, Richard. *Superior Illusions*. Toronto: Natural Heritage Books, 1998.

Raffan, James. *Bark, Skin and Cedar: Exploring the Canoe in the Canadian Experience*. Toronto: HarperCollins, 1999.

Ray, Arthur J. *The Canadian Fur Trade in the Industrial Age*. Toronto: University of Toronto Press, 1990.

———. *I Have Lived Here Since the World Began*. Toronto: Key Porter, 1996.

———. *Indians in the Fur Trade*. Toronto: University of Toronto Press, 1974.

Ray, Arthur J., and Donald Freeman. *"Give Us Good Measure": An Economic Analysis of Relations Between the Indians and the Hudson's Bay Company Before 1763*. Toronto: University of Toronto Press, 1978.

Reid, Anna. *The Shaman's Coat: A Native History of Siberia*. London: Weidenfeld and Nicolson, 2002.

Rich, E.E. *The Fur Trade and the Northwest to 1857*. Toronto: McClelland and Stewart, 1967.

Roberts, Kenneth G., and Philip Shackleton. *The Canoe*. Toronto: Macmillan, 1983.

Rogers, Edward S., and Donald B. Smith. *Aboriginal Ontario: Historical Perspectives of the First Nations*. Toronto: Dundurn Press, 1994.

Schrenck, Theresa. *The Voice of the Crane Echoes Afar: The Sociopolitical Organization of the Lake Superior Ojibwa, 1640–1855*. New York: Garland, 1997.

Sevareid, Eric. *Canoeing with the Cree*. St. Paul: Minnesota Historical Society Press, 1968.

Simpson, George. *Simpson's Athabasca Journal*. Toronto: Hudson's Bay Record Society, 1938.

———. *Simpson's 1828 Journey to the Columbia*. Toronto: Hudson's Bay Record Society, 1947.

Steele, Ian K. *Warpaths*. New York: Oxford University Press, 1994.

Steinbruch, Jean. *The Yellowknife Journal*. Winnipeg: Nuage Editions, 1999.

Taylor, Garth. *Canoe Construction in a Cree Cultural Tradition*. Canadian Ethnology Service Paper 64. Ottawa: Canadian Museum of Civilization, 1980.

Thompson, David. *Columbia Journals*, edited by Barbara Belyea. Montreal: McGill–Queen's University Press, 1994.

Trigger, Bruce. *The Children of Aetaentsic: A History of the Huron People to 1660*. Montreal: McGill–Queen's University Press, 1976.

Trudel, Marcel. *The Beginnings of New France, 1524–1663*. Toronto: McClelland and Stewart, 1973.

Tyrrell, J.B., ed. *David Thompson's Narrative*. Toronto: Champlain Society, 1916.

Van Kirk, Sylvia. *"Many Tender Ties": Women in Fur Trade Society, 1670–1870*. Winnipeg: Watson & Dwyer, 1980.

Voorhis, Ernest. *The Historic Forts and Trading Posts of the French Regime and of the English Fur Trading Companies*. Ottawa: Canada Department of the Interior, 1930.

Wallace, W. Stewart. *The Peddlers from Quebec*. Toronto: Ryerson Press, 1954.

Warren, Graham, and David Gidmark. *Canoe Paddles*. Toronto: Firefly Books, 2001.

Warren, William W. *History of the Ojibway People*. St. Paul: Minnesota Historical Society Press, 1984.

White, Richard. *The Middle Ground*. Cambridge: Cambridge University Press, 1991.

Wishart, David J. *The Fur Trade of the American West, 1807–1840*. Lincoln: University of Nebraska Press, 1979.

Index

Abenaki (St. Francis and other), 50, 51; canoes, 48, 125, 142; models, 24, 51, 52, 53, 54, 55, 56, 57, 58

Adney, Edwin Tappan: articles by, 13–14, 18, 130–33; *Bark Canoes and Skin Boats of North America,* 17, 142; on Beothuk, 45; birchbark thesis, 139; birth of son, 15; on canoe decoration, 143; on canoe regions, 84, 135, 136–39; as canoeist, 14; commercial art and murals, 15, 16; comparisons by of world canoes, 104, 108, 114; correspondence, 18–19; death, 25, 142; on "decadence," 34, 79; early years, 11–13; on factory-built canoes, 142; favorite canoe, 50; financial difficulties, 16, 18, 20; illustrations by, 11, 13, 14, 15, 16, 19, 23, 24, 140; Klondike years, 25, 94; and Lionel Judah relationship, 19–21, 22; manuscript, 16, 17, 18, 22, 25, 142; and Mariners' Museum purchase, 22; marriage, 12, 14–15; McGill connection, 18, 19–21; meets Peter Jo, 12–13; methodology and research, 98, 119, 135, 139; migration theory, 108, 114; Missinaibi expedition, 20, 21; Montreal years, 15–16, 18; Native advocacy, 16, 22, 25; New Brunswick years, 15, 21; New York years, 15; pictures of, 10, 25, 26; on qualities of birchbark, 104, 120; Rupert House visit, 72; search for fur-trade canoes, 127

Adney, Francis Glenn: and Adney's manuscript material, 25; on Adney's relationship with Judah, 21; birth of, 15; on father's personality, 21; music training and career, 19; and sale of Adney's models, 22

Adney, Mary, 11, 12

Adney, Minnie Bell (Sharp), 12, 21, 14–16

Adney, Ruth Clementine Shaw, 11

Adney, W.H.G., 11

Africa, 135

Ainu, 108, 112, 113; canoes, 113, 135; models, 112, 113

Alaska: as canoe region, 84, 136, 137. *See also* Northwest

Aleutian Islands, 108, 113

Algonquin, 50, 53; birchbark roll, 139; canoes, 48, 123; gunwale lashing, 129; headboards, 128; models, 56, 57, 58, 59, 60, 61, 126; stempieces, 128

Amazon River, 117

American Museum of Natural History, 31, 113, 114, 115

Amur River canoes, 104, 105, 107, 108, 109, 110, 111, 135, 137–39; models, 107, 109, 110, 111

Asia: canoes, 104, 107, 108, 109, 110, 111, 112, 113, 114, 115; uses of birchbark in, 136

Athapascan canoes, 89; models, 98, 99, 100, 101, 114

Atwin, Frank, 12, 13

Austin, A., 52

Australia, 135

Barbeau, Marius, 18

bark: replaced by canvas, 123; qualities, 80, 82, 83, 91; types, 135. *See also* basswood, beech, birchbark, cedar, chestnut, cottonwood, elm, hickory, oak, purple heart, spruce

bark canoe: capacity, 120; comparisons, 84, 87, 104; regions, 135; South American, 116–19; steps to building, 17. *See also* specific barks

basswood, 135; bark canoe model, 80

Bastard canoe, 122 (model), 141

Bay of Chaleur, 31

Bear, Peter, 36, 40

Bear Island region, 55, 124, 126

Beaver people: craft built by, 137

beech bark, 116, 135; canoe model, 116

Beothuk, 28, 45; canoes, 16; models, 45, 46, 47, 48, 49

Bering Sea and Strait, 108, 139

Bernard, Matt, 57

birchbark: alliance, 141–42; kayaks, 103; properties, 73, 97, 99, 104, 120, 135–36; other uses, 136

birchbark canoes: 135–39; of Amur River, 104; comparisons, 104, 107, 108, 109, 110, 112, 114; consistency among, 139; disappearance, 72, 142; flotillas, 140; and kayaks, 103; Maliseet, 13; nails introduced, 29, 96, 120; replacement of, 72, 142; sizes, 141; splash-guard, 85; technology, 120

birchbark canoe models: Abenaki and Abenaki-type, 24 (sketch), 51, 52, 53, 54, 55, 56, 57; Ainu, 112, 122; Algonquin, 58, 59, 60, 61, 122; Amur River, 106, 109, 110, 111; Athapascan, 98, 99, 101; Beothuk, 45, 46, 47, 48, 49; Carrier, 102; Chipewyan, 85, 86, 87, 88; Dogrib, 90, 91; E. Ojibwa, 64, 65, 66, 67; Gwich'in, 24 (sketch), 94, 95, 97; Hudson's Bay, 124; Iroquois, 121; Malemut, 103; Maliseet, 34, 35, 36, 37, 38, 39; Mi'kmaq, 29, 30, 31; Montagnais, 68, 69; Naskapi crooked, 70, 71; N. Cree, 89; Passamaquoddy, 43 (river), 44 (ocean), 44 (painted); Restigouche, 31, 32; Slavey, 92, 93; Têtes de Boule 62, 63, 125, 126, 127; W. Cree, 78; W. Ojibwa, 76, 77, 78

Bois Fort Reserve, 76, 78

Boonesborough style, 81

British Columbia: canoes, 104, 105, 106, 136, 137–39. *See also* Northwest region

British Guiana Museum, 118

Camsell, Charles, 92

Canadian Canoe Museum, 18, 57

Canadian Museum of Civilization, 18, 29, 32, 46, 53, 55, 76, 78, 82, 86, 87, 88, 90, 91, 106

Canadian Pacific Railway, 67, 70, 102, 126

Canadian Shield, 135

canoes: canoe art, 16; routes, 144–45; shapes, 138. *See also* bark canoes, canvas canoes, decorations, specific barks

canvas: as bark replacement, 123; canoes: 33, 42, 142; as covering, 69

canvas canoe models: Cree (Hudson's Bay), 123; E. Cree, 72; Gwich'in, 96; Kootenay sturgeon-nose, 105; Maliseet, 33; Naskapi crooked, 70; Passamaquoddy, 42

cargo canoes, 87

Carib dugout canoes, 119

Carrier canoes and craft, 104, 137; models, 102

Cartier, Jacques, 19, 140

cedar-strip and cedar/canvas canoes, 142; qualities of white cedar, 137

Champlain, Samuel de, 82, 139, 140

Chapelle, Howard, 11, 25; *Bark Canoes and Skin Boats of North America* (Adney and), 17, 142

Chapman, Frank M., 11

Chase, William Merritt, 11

Château de Ramezay Museum, 38, 24, 52, 78

chestnut bark, 135

Chicago, 141

Child, Edwin B.: painting of Adney by, 25

Chilton, Willie, 62

China. *See* Amur River

Chipewa, 50; Chipewyan canoe models, 85, 86, 87, 88; craft built by, 137

Christopherson, Louis, 16, 121, 126

Clarke, Dr. George F., 21

cottonwood bark, 135

Cox, Kenyon, 11

cradleboards, 137

Crerar, T.A., 18

Cree: canoes, 15 (paddles), 88 (sails); major Cree groups, 50, 68, 71; models, 89, 72, 73, 74, 75, 123

crooked canoe: 70

Currie, Sir Arthur, 20

Dawson, George M., 124

decorations: beaver and leaf, 36; bow and stern, 143; crescent moon, 31; disk (rayed), 121, 142, 143; dots, 69; Dutch-influenced, 121, 143; eagle, 44; eight-point star, 31, 36; fiddlehead, 36, 37; hoops, 36; patches, 75; spirals, 121; tadpole, 12, 13; zigzag, 31, 36, 37, 85, 93

Denis, Soisin, 44

Detroit (Fort Pontchartrain), 141
Dogrib canoes and craft, 85, 86, 103, 137; models, 90, 91
dugout canoes: Athapascan, 114; Carib and Seminole, 119; Yukaghir, 114
dupskodegun, 36, 136
Dutch traders: influence, 121, 143

East Coast: birchbark as trade item in 136; canoes, 14, 28–49, 84, 87; Native peoples, 28
Eastern Woodlands: as canoe region, 136–37; canoes, 50–83, 84; fur trade, 50; map, 134; Native peoples, 50
Edison Institute, 18
elm bark, 135; canoes, 80; models, 82, 83
eucalyptus canoe, 135
Europe: as bark canoe region, 135
Eustan, Chief, 106
Express canoe, 19 (illustr.), 124 (model)

family canoes, 87
Field Museum of Natural History, 16, 18
Fladmark, Knut, 108
Forrester, Colonel E., 104
Fort Chipewyan: as fur-trade focal point, 84
Fort Churchill, 88
forts (fur-trade frontier map), 144–45
France: colonizing by, 140
fur trade: Adney's knowledge, 25; background, 13, 16, 84; canoe routes, 144–45; canoes, 120–27, 140 (sketch), 142, 143; and Native peoples, 50, 63, 89, 140–41; and North canoe, 66; posts, 64, 70, 71; and transporting of birchbark, 99

Geological Survey of Canada, 70, 71, 72, 91, 92, 124; canoes used by, 142
Gilman, Henry, 67
Golden Lake, Ontario: as canoe-building center, 54, 57, 58, 59, 61, 122
Goldi, 109
Grand Lake Victoria, 16, 62
Grand Portage, 141
Great Lakes, 139, 141; Champlain's journey to, 139; Erie, 141; Huron, 57, 58, 141; Superior, 64, 66, 67
Great Peace (1701), 141
grooves (identification), 98
gumming: women's role in (illustr.), 137
gunwale (illustr.), 16, 129
Guyanese canoes, 118, 119
Gwich'in: canoes and craft, 84, 103, 137; models, 24 (sketch), 94, 95, 96, 97; territory, 103

Han people: craft built by, 137
Hare people: craft built by, 137
headboard: view of, 128

Hearne, Samuel, 85
Henry Ford Museum of Transportation and Industry, 16
Heye, George, 16, 18
hickory bark, 135; canoe model, 80
Hill, Frederick F., 21–22
Hill, Nola: description of Adney by, 22–25
Hopkins, Frances Ann, 16, 124
Hudson Bay, 72, 137, 88, 89
Hudson's Bay Company, 15, 16; blanket, 88; canoes used by, 19, 55, 60, 121, 122, 123, 124, 125, 126, 142; and Native peoples, 89, 143
Huloff, William Jr., 59
hunting canoes, 85, 86, 87, 137; birch-bark used in (photo), 139; Yukaghir, 115. See also Beothuk
huskies, 103

Idaho: canoe region, 136, 137–39; canoes, 106. See also Northwest region
Imperial Academy of Sciences, 110
Innu, 50, 68. See also Montagnais
Inuit kayaks, 25, 84, 86, 98, 114; asymmetry, 95; birchbark and sealskin, 103; frame, 137
Iroquois, 120, 143; canoe colors, 143; canoe models, 81, 120, 82, 83; stem-piece, 128; threat to trading alliance, 140, 141–42

James, William Curtis, 113
James Bay, 64, 141
Japan: aboriginal people, 108, 112, 113, 135; canoe region, 135
Jenness, Diamond, 18, 19, 22
Jo, Peter, 12–13, 39, 130; pictured, 133
Josephs, Tomah, 34
Judah, Lionel: 21 (photo); relationship with Adney, 19–21, 22

Kamchatka Peninsula, 108, 114
Kane, Paul, 16
Kaska people: craft built by, 137
kayaks. See Inuit kayaks
Kelley, David, 108
Kennebec, 28, 50, 51. See also Abenaki
Klondike: Adney's sketches and travels, 13–15, 23, 25, 94; canoes, 14
Kootenay canoes, 104, 136, 137–39; models, 105, 106; and those of Amur Valley, 139
Kurile Islands, 108

Labrador. See Eastern Woodlands
Lac St. Jean, 67
lakes: Abitibi, 122; Athabasca, 84; Barrière, 16, 62; Great Bear Lake, 92; Great Slave Lake, 90, 91; Kipawa, 122; Nipigon, 77; Red Lake, 77; Shuswap Lake, 104; Temagami, 55, 124, 126;

Winnipeg, 66. See also Great Lakes
Lena River (Russia), 110, 111
Long Nose canoes, 126
Low, A.P., 71

Mackenzie Basin, 136, 137
Maine, 28; cedar/canvas canoes, 142. See also East Coast, Eastern Woodlands
Malemut canoes: birchbark, 13; models, 102
Maliseet: Adney lithograph of, 14; canoes, 19, 28; dupskodegun, 136; models, 20–21, 33, 34, 35, 36, 37, 38, 39, 41, 48, 50, 51; racing traditions, 38; ribs (canoe), 129. See also Abenaki
Manitoba: Inuit lands, 50. See also Eastern Woodlands
Manitoulin Island, 58
Maniwaki, Quebec: as canoe-building center, 53, 54, 57, 59, 122, 126, 142
Mariners' Museum, 11, 21–22; acquisition of Adney's manuscript, 25; Adney's papers at, 16, 25; Adney's visit to, 22, 25; collection, 40, 143; sale of Adney's models to, 22
Mason, Bill, 135
Mason, J.A., 91
Mason, Otis T., 106, 109, 111
McCord Museum, 31, 56, 75, 60, 100, 101
McGill University, 18, 19–21, 22
McPhee, John: Survival of the Bark Canoe, 15
Michel, Antoine, 53
Michigan. See Eastern Woodlands
Michilimacinac, 141
migration: canoe types (map), 134; to N. America, 108, 109, 113, 114, 139
Mi'kmaq: canoes, 45; fishing among, 30; models, 29, 30, 31, 32; racing traditions, 38
Minnesota. See Eastern Woodlands
Missinaibi fur-trade canoes, 124
missionaries, 141–42
Mitchinini, 64
Mitledge, William, 21
Mohawk: paddling speed, 124
Montagnais (Innu), 50, 68: canoes, 45, 129; models, 68, 69; tradition, 69
Montana, 106. See also Northwest region
Montreal canoe, 13, 122, 141
moosehide canoe model, 41
Moulton, Noel, 41
murianara tree. See purple heart
Museum of the American Indian, 16, 18

Nadoe Chiman canoe, 125
nails, 29, 96, 120
Naskapi, 50, 68, 71; canoe models, 70, 71
Native peoples and cultures: Adney's interest in, 16, 22, 25, 135; Europeans and, 120, 140–41; Hudson's Bay

Company and, 89; of northern North America (map), 8; relationship between canoe and, 135; uses of birch-bark, 135–36; westward migrations of (map), 114. *See also* individual entries

New Brunswick: Adney's years in, 15, 21; canoes, 29, 31, 142; Native peoples, 28. *See also* East Coast

New France, 140–42

New York State. *See* Eastern Woodlands

New Zealand bark canoe region, 135

Newfoundland, 28. *See also* Beothuk

Nishimura, Shinji, 107

North canoe, 122, 141

Northwest Company, 121

Northwest Passage, 140

Northwest region: and Asian canoes (comparisons), 104–107, 108, 109, 110, 112, 114; canoes, 84–103, 104, 105, 136, 137; Native peoples, 84

Northwest Territories, 92. *See also* Northwest region

Nova Scotia: canoes built in, 30, 31. *See also* East Coast

oak bark, 135

ocean-going canoes: journeys in, 47; of Passamaquoddy, 44. *See also* Beothuk

ocher (red): qualities and uses, 48, 68

Ojibwa: canoe models, 57, 64, 65, 66, 67, 76, 77, 78, 79 (skiff), 126; canoe ribs, 129; gunwales, 129; headboards, 128; territory, 50, 66

Ontario, 50. *See also* Eastern Woodlands; Golden Lake; Peterborough

Orinoco region canoes, 135

paddle guard (pegged), 122

paddling speed, 124

Panadis, Nicola, 51, 52

Papineau, Louis-Joseph, 61

Passamaquoddy, 28; canoes, 142; models, 42, 43, 44

Peabody, G.A., 43

Peabody Essex Museum, 11, 14, 20, 25

Peabody Museum, Harvard University, 34, 43, 44, 65, 67, 69, 89, 98

Peck, Edward, 73

Peck, Hugh, 75

Peck, Mrs. Edward, 99

Penobscot, 28, 50, 51; canoe (illustr.), 15

Peru, 117

Peterborough, Ontario: and cedar/canvas canoes, 142

Pictou (Picto), Joseph, 31

Pitiguay, Chief Charles, 125

Pitiguay, Testibaldi, 62

Pond, Peter, 84

poplar: use of in Yukaghir canoes, 115

portages (longest), 84

Porter, J.B., 60

Prince Edward Island. *See* East Coast

purple heart bark canoes, 135; models, 117, 118, 119

Quayshish, Michael, 21; canoe of (photo), 21

Quebec (Gaspé region). *See* East Coast

Quebec. Native peoples, 28, 50. *See also* Eastern Woodlands

railroads, 142

Reed, Hayter, 102

reindeer herders' canoes, 110

rib of canoe (illustr.), 16, 129

rivers and river regions (N. American): Albany, 72; Bear, 30, 31, 40; Churchill, 89; Fraser, 98, 102, 104; Gatineau, 56, 126; Great Whale, 70; Hudson, 143; Liard, 100; Mackenzie, 89, 93; Maliseet, 28; Manouan, 62; Missinaibi, 20, 21, 64; Mississippi/Missouri, 139, 141–42; Mohawk, 143; Natashquan, 70; North, 88; Ottawa, 50, 62, 122, 126; Penobscot, 41; Restigouche, 32; Saint John, 28, 32, 34, 36, 37, 38, 39; St. Croix, 28; St. Lawrence, 38, 50, 69, 125, 136, 139, 140; St. Maurice, 62, 63, 125, 126; Thompson, 104; Winisk, 72, 74, 75, 78; Yukon, 95, 103, 114

Roop, Kendell, 117

Roosevelt, Theodore, 11

Royal Military College, 15, 16

Russia. *See* Amur River; Lena River; Siberia

Russian Imperial Museum, 109, 111

Sacobie, Frank, 34

sails and sailing, 29, 77, 88

Salish: canoes, 136, 137–39

Sapir, Edward, 18

Sapporo Museum, 112

Sarazin family, 54, 58, 122

Saskatchewan. *See* Eastern Woodlands

Saulteaux, 50, 66

Scott, Adam Sherriff, 16

Sea of Okhotsk, 105, 108

sealskin (in kayaks), 103

Secani people: craft built by, 137

Seminole dugout canoes, 119

Sharp, Francis Peabody, 12

sheathing, 16

shoes (canoe), 39

Shuswap canoe models, 104

Siberia: bark craft, 18, 135; dugout canoes, 114; umiaks, 108

Simpson, Dr. J.C., 20

Simpson, Sir George, 124

Slavey: canoe models, 92, 93; craft built by, 137

sleds, 37

Smithsonian Institution, 16, 18, 106, 109, 110, 117

snowshoes, 137

Solis, John, 36

South American canoes: 116–19, 121; models, 116, 117, 118, 119; regions, 135

Speck, F.G., 68

spruce bark, 40, 73, 74, 135

spruce bark canoe models: Athapascan, 100; Cree, 73, 74, 75; Kootenay sturgeon-nose, 106; Maliseet, 40; Shuswap sturgeon-nose, 104

St. Francis Abenaki. *See* Abenaki

St. Lawrence River: trade fairs, 140, 141. *See also* rivers

Steele, J.B., 117

Stefansson, Vilhjalmur, 253

stempieces: view of, 128

Strathcona Ethnological Museum (McGill), 19–20

Tahlton people: craft built by, 137

Tanana people: craft built by, 14, 137

tanning: frost-tanned process, 41

Têtes de Boule, 21 (photo), 50; canoe models, 62, 63, 125, 127; canoes, 136 (designs), 127 (paddles); as fur-trade canoe builders, 12, 63, 127. *See also* Abenaki

Tierra del Fuego, 135

toboggans, 137

Trois-Rivières: as canoe-building center, 62, 141

Tuchone people: craft built by, 137

Tungus people, 109, 110, 111

umiaks, 108

voyaging canoes, 141

Walcott fund, 98

war canoes (Iroquois), 82, 83

Washington State: as canoe region, 136, 137–39. *See also* Northwest region

Waugh, F.W., 53, 70

Wet'suwet'en (Carrier) canoes and craft, 104, 137; models, 102

Wheeler, D.E., 90

White Duck, Peter, 56

Whymper, Frederick, 94

wigwams, 136

wild rice: harvesting, 66, 78, 79

Wisconsin. *See* Eastern Woodlands

women: role of (illustr.), 137

woodskin bark canoes (S. American), 119

wulegessis, 16 (illustr.), 36, 39

Yahgan canoes, 116

Yakut (Sakha) people, 111

Yellowknife people: craft built by, 137

Yezo Island: as bark canoe region, 135

Yukaghir canoe models, 114, 115

Yukon: as canoe region, 136, 137. *See also* Klondike; Northwest region